APR – 4 2019

W9-BKG-281

# MARVEL STUD10S
## THE FIRST TEN YEARS

In 2008, Tony Stark made his first Iron Man suit. Shortly after, Nick Fury told Stark that he had "become part of a bigger universe..."

In the years since then, amazing new places – like Wakanda – have been discovered, new Avengers teams have assembled, strange new Guardians of the Galaxy have formed, and old friends have had their own Civil War.

During this time, the hunt for all six Infinity Stones has continued. Now, all the worlds, all the characters, and all the Stones have finally come together.

In this special Collector's Edition, we look back over the characters, locations, Easter Eggs, and rich history behind the Marvel Cinematic Universe.

THE OFFICIAL MARVEL MOVIE SPECIALS
*Thor: Ragnarok*
*Black Panther*
*Avengers: Infinity War*
*Ant-Man and the Wasp*
*Captain Marvel*

Also available:
*Black Panther: The Official Movie Companion*

**TITAN EDITORIAL**
**Editor** Jonathan Wilkins
**Senior Editor** Martin Eden
**Assistant Editors**
Tolly Maggs & Jake Devine
**Senior Designer** Andrew Leung
**Art Director** Oz Browne
**Contributors** Mark McKenzie-Ray, David Leach, Dan Boultwood, Nick Jones
**Senior Production Controller** Jackie Flook
**Production Controller** Peter James
**Senior Sales Manager** Steve Tothill
**Subscriptions Executive** Tony Ho
**Direct Sales & Marketing Manager** Ricky Claydon

**Advertising Assistant** Bella Hoy
**Commercial Manager** Michelle Fairlamb
**Circulation Executive** Frankie Hallam
**U.S. Advertising Manager** Jeni Smith
**Publishing Manager** Darryl Tothill
**Publishing Director** Chris Teather
**Operations Director** Leigh Baulch
**Executive Director** Vivian Cheung
**Publisher** Nick Landau

**DISTRIBUTION**
**US Newsstand** Total
Publisher Services, Inc.
John Dziewiatkowski, 630-851-7683

**US Distribution** Curtis Circulation Company, Ingram Periodicals
**US Direct Sales Market**
Diamond Comic Distributors
For more info on advertising contact adinfo@titanemail.com

*Marvel Studios: The First 10 years* published December 2018 by Titan Magazines, a division of Titan Publishing Group Limited, 144 Southwark Street, London SE1 0UP.
For sale in the US and Canada.
Printed in Canada by Transcontinental Interglobe

Thank you to Shiho Tilley, Beatrice Osman, and Eugene Paraszczuk at Disney for all their help.

Titan Authorized User. No part of this publication may be reproduced, stored in a retrival system, or transmitted, in any form or by any means, without the prior written permission of the publisher. A CIP catalogue record for this title is available from the British Library.
10 9 8 7 6 5 4 3 2 1

# CONTENTS

## PHASE ONE

## PHASE TWO

## PHASE THREE

INTERVIEW

## KEVIN FEIGE

# Building a Universe

The President of Marvel Studios celebrates the Marvel Cinematic Universe after ten years, reflecting on how far it's come and examining what has made it work so well.

How essential is the chemistry between actors when casting for the Marvel films?
We always cast for the movie we're making, but we also have an eye on the future. So when we were casting Chris Pratt, we needed the best Star-Lord, but at the same time, we said, "We need somebody who one day might go toe to toe with Robert Downey Jr." On the very first day of *Avengers: Infinity War* there was Robert, Chris Pratt, Tom Holland, and it was pretty amazing! There have been a handful of times in our ten years here at Marvel Studios where we have had to just stop for a second and pinch ourselves. That was one of those moments.

How do you know if a character is going to connect with audiences?
We believe that what we're working on has value. The risks and creative chances that we're taking are in service to creating something an audience will respond to, something unique and different. I believe deeply that's what filmgoers want – to be surprised and to have expectations exceeded. You don't know until it's out, but all we've done since Phase One is go with our gut.

How important has Thanos been to the Marvel Cinematic Universe as the main villain?
Thanos has been lurking in the shadows with a desire to obtain these Infinity Stones, which has played a big part in our other films. We've introduced the Tesseract, revealed to be the Space Stone; the Mind Stone, which came out of Loki's scepter and then went into Vision's forehead; and the Time Stone: the Eye of Agamotto that Doctor Strange wears is an Infinity Stone itself! And of course the Guardians dealt with the Power Stone.

So these storytelling devices that we've seeded into every film will continue to play a part and come together. We've been teasing this for six years. That's a long time to tease

something cinematically before paying it off. Thanos has to be the greatest villain in our movies.

What made the Russos the right choice to take the MCU to the next level in *Avengers: Infinity War*?
We were midway through production on *Civil War* and we saw the amazing job that Anthony and Joe were doing, handling all these different characters and telling this unique storyline. We could be on a set with a thousand crewmembers, but the directors put that aside and think about the experience people are gonna have in the cinema seats. Joe and Anthony do that expertly.

Will the Quantum Realm play a bigger part in the future?
At the end of *Ant-Man* we followed Scott Lang into the Quantum Realm for the first time. We were beginning to peel back the onion that would later be completely peeled back in *Doctor Strange* as we go into the multiverse. So that was our little test into that.

But now the Quantum Realm is a whole other territory that we can play with to tell our stories. This Quantum Realm is much larger than we ever imagined, and there are all sorts of adventures to be had at that level, which perhaps we will explore in another film.

Has there been a moment over the last ten years where you realized what you were setting up was going to be a success?
I think it was *The Avengers*. The success of *Iron Man* was amazing. That gave us the confidence to do another *Iron Man* film, a *Captain America* film, and to introduce Thor. The success of *The Avengers* taught us that the audience really gets what we're doing, and really enjoys the cross-pollination of all of these different film series. And the audience told us unequivocally they were with us. That allowed us to plot out everything that we've done since then, and everything specifically building to *Infinity War*.

# Producing 10 Years of Marvel Movies

The Co-President of Marvel Studios, Louis D'Esposito has been working with Kevin Feige as executive producer on every Marvel Studios movie to date, starting with 2008's *Iron Man*. Here he looks back on a decade of moviemaking.

**Why was the casting of Iron Man such an important step in establishing the Marvel Cinematic Universe?**
I think casting Robert Downey Jr. as Tony Stark was probably our most important casting decision because it informed everything else. Having Robert Downey Jr. has been absolutely fantastic, not only for the *Iron Man* franchise but for the whole Marvel Cinematic Universe.

**Has it been fun watching the character evolve?**
It's been interesting watching Tony Stark *and* Robert Downey Jr. evolve. They're one and the same. It's really incredible watching an actor of that caliber develop and change from film to film. A lot of Tony Stark might have been just glib one-liners but there's an emotional resonance. His relationship with the other Avengers, Pepper Potts, and most importantly with himself and how that's developed has been quite extraordinary.

**What are Robert Downey Jr.'s greatest strengths?**
Robert can get away with saying a lot, and people still like him. He's very likeable. Tony Stark goes from being quite a selfish man in the original *Iron Man* to being

willing to sacrifice himself for the greater good further down the line. That's over the course of 22 films. That kind of evolution can only be done in something like this. Tony Stark hasn't been in every film, but he's been mentioned in a lot of them. He's had his lion's share of screen time. He's quite remarkable. Watching him on set is amazing because he really understands the story. He likes to adlib, and he's always on point. He's always serving the story. Even when he's taking some liberties with the script, he's always making it even better.

**What has Robert brought to the franchise as a whole?**
I think Robert's become a bit more reflective about his work on these films. Robert is such a great actor. He really needed *Iron Man*. He wanted to do that film, and we really needed him. Now he takes it in his stride and with such confidence. He's a mentor to all the other actors. He's like the Godfather on set, taking care of everyone. You go to him with your problems and he helps find solutions. We've watched him go from being the solitary hero in *Iron Man* to the financial head of the Avengers. I would argue that Captain America is the tactical leader, but Tony Stark is the intellectual leader from a science perspective.

**How many visual effects shots are there on *Iron Man* compared to *Avengers: Infinity War*?**
We started with 487 on *Iron Man* and we finished with 823. For *Avengers: Infinity War* it's over 3,100. That's almost every shot.

**The culmination of this ten-year story has been a long time coming. Is it good to finally pay things off?**
Yes. We've been teasing Thanos as being the ultimate villain since *The Avengers* back in 2012. Marvel Comics readers will understand why he deserves such a build-up. He is very imposing and formidable. He's basically an eco-terrorist. He wants to eliminate 50 percent of the universe, arbitrarily, to save the other 50 percent. On his home planet of Titan he noticed the overpopulation and starvation starting to happen and he proposed this as a solution. Titan did self-

destruct, so now he's trying to save the universe. So what Thanos decides to do is to get the six Infinity Stones so he can snap his fingers and arbitrarily get rid of 50 percent of the universe. It is quite a moving moment because we've never seen the Marvel heroes really lose. It's quite emotional to see that happen.

**Is it important to make audiences relate to this?**
I think it's a relatable situation because there *is* overpopulation. I don't think anyone on Earth is proposing the same fix as Thanos. But how do you handle that? Human beings will overcome that problem – we will figure out a way. What makes Thanos so great is that his conviction and his belief is that this is the only way. There is no other solution. He's seen it firsthand on his planet, and he's doing what needs to be done for the greater good. So with

05

> ## "Conflict is what moves the story. Seeing the interaction and the conflict [between the characters] is truly amazing."

that kind of conviction and that kind of belief it really makes him a powerful villain. The Avengers are trying to save everyone. They don't want to lose one life. So they are at polar opposites with their enemy. There are some people like Drax who are out for revenge. Gamora is out for revenge against her father. Drax's wife and daughter were murdered. So you have a mixture of revenge and the Avengers wanting to protect not only Earth, but the rest of the universe from this tyrant. I think what also makes Thanos relatable is that he's played by Josh Brolin, who brings a sense of reality to the character. His relationship with Gamora is truly a father/daughter relationship. And even though no one has

ever met anyone like Thanos, the audience can relate to a father talking to his daughter and they can relate to a politician or a president wanting to offer a solution to some impending doom. His determination is very relatable.

**Do you think the cast elevate each other?**
Our sets are like sporting events! It's like when you have the Lakers playing the Celtics and both teams raise their game. Every game is like a playoff game. It's the same thing with our actors on set. They elevate each other. We have some of the best actors in the world today working together. But a lot of times there's conflict between the characters. Conflict is what moves the story. Seeing that interaction between the characters and that conflict between them is truly amazing. We take it for granted when we're back in the office. We're looking at dailies, but when we get on set and witness it firsthand, you see the actors at their best. It's really amazing. It's like when Joe DiMaggio would catch a baseball and run with it with such fluidity and ease. That's the way they perform. It's at the highest level.

**Was it a deliberate choice for the Marvel Studios films to be different genres?**
We have done that on some films. For instance, with *Captain America: The Winter Soldier* we wanted to make a political thriller, so we modeled it after that type of film. The first *Ant-Man* was a heist movie. You

**01** Iron Man soars into action, setting the tone for ten years of Marvel Studios movies. (See previous spread)

**02** Thanos reaches his endgame in *Avengers: Infinity War*.

**03** Behind-the-scenes action on *Ant-Man*.

**04** Star-Lord – ready for his close-up in *Guardians of the Galaxy*.

**05** A complex action sequence is filmed as Georges Batroc squares up to Captain America in *Captain America: The Winter Soldier*.

06

look at some of the tropes from those types of films and adapt them. First and foremost, we want to tell the story in its simplest form so people that haven't seen our films can understand it. The people that have seen our films can really enjoy some of the callbacks. The challenge for *Infinity War* was: "How do you tell our most complicated story to date in the simplest form? How do you give that many actors their due?" There are a lot of storylines that have to be finished by the end of the film and we only have a certain period of time to tell it in.

**How much planning goes into making the movies appeal to diehard fans and casual moviegoers?**
It's all planned out. You can hear how the story is complicated. So how do you distill it into its simplest form so it becomes enjoyable and you don't feel like you're taking your SAT tests when you go to see the film? We always say, what if someone's never seen a Marvel movie before? How do they understand the Quantum Realm? Well, they understand that it's a place where time is different. You didn't have to see *Ant-Man* where we first explained that concept. The audience that has seen *Ant-Man* knows that the Quantum Realm is where Hank Pym was looking for his wife for the longest time. So it just becomes a little bit more enjoyable for the avid fan. The casual

## "The Quantum Realm is where Hank Pym was looking for his wife for the longest time."

viewers have heard of these terms, so they can pick it up. We've been fortunate that we have such committed filmmakers here that are mainly all working on separate projects. They're all connected, and we all contribute to each other's projects.

**Was *Captain America: Civil War* a particularly important film for the franchise?**
*Civil War* was one of the biggest comics. It was a story we wanted to tell. It was about identification in the comics, so it was a little bit different in the film. At the beginning of *Captain America: Civil War* I don't think we were considering directors for *Avengers 3* and *4* at that time. We didn't know if we were going to film them together or not. I don't think we'd ever

**06** Chris Evans and Samuel L. Jackson perform on a green screen set during the filming of *Captain America: The Winter Soldier.*

**07** Aaron Taylor-Johnson as Quicksilver on the set of the second Avengers movie: *Age of Ultron.*

**08** Chadwick Boseman goes before the camera as T'Challa in *Black Panther.*

**09** Benedict Cumberbatch on set as the Sorceror Supreme in *Doctor Strange.*

do that again. It sounded fantastic in the room at the time. You have to do that because of the actors. There are so many actors and to go back in another year and try to get them all together again would be really difficult. It has been a daunting task but the production crew has been absolutely amazing. [Producer] Mike Grillo and his team have been managing this tremendous cast and all the scheduling problems you can imagine. The Russos bringing together the storylines in *Civil War* was quite a feat. It was a complicated ending because two of the most beloved characters fought each other at the end. How can we make the audience swallow that?

It's hard because we go to the movies for a lot of reasons, but I think we go to see these big franchise films for a laugh and to forget our troubles. We like to leave with a satisfying ending because we put ourselves in the shoes of the protagonists. People want to live vicariously through these characters, so when they fight each other, it's quite disturbing. I know a lot of people were affected by that. The Russos had to juggle complicated storylines from previous films, especially with the Bucky storyline and the death of Tony's parents. I think they're formidable directors. They're as hard-working as anyone that we've ever worked with. They love these characters. They love this genre. After *Civil War*, it became obvious to Kevin and I that they're the people for the job.

**How crucial is it that the audience really cares about these characters?**
It's most fun and rewarding when you see people laugh or tear up or get tense at a scene, or upset because of a conflict when their favorite people are fighting with each other. I think that's our strength and will continue to be. When you look at our films, they are all different. *Thor: Ragnarok* was reviewed as a fully-fledged comedy. *Black Panther* has got some fun moments, but it's a lot more serious. *Infinity War* is even more serious because the stakes are much greater. It brings everyone together. After that, there's *Ant-Man and the Wasp*, which is a great fun family film. We try to be different every time. We want our stories to resonate from different perspectives. There's always got to be a little bit of humor – I think we're known for that. Some movies need to be more serious than others. That's why we hired Taika Waititi for *Thor: Ragnorok*, because we knew what the tone of that film should be. Chris Hemsworth has really grown into a great comedic actor. Not only is he great at comedy, he's great at emotion.

**What can fans look forward to next?**
*Captain Marvel* is up next. It's set in the 1990s. Captain Marvel interacts with Nick Fury, but Nick Fury at this point in his life is not the Nick Fury that you know and love. He is not the director of S.H.I.E.L.D. at this point. He thinks his job is a dead end, but meeting Captain Marvel changes all that for him...

# IRON MAN (2008)

## DIRECTED BY: JON FAVREAU

STARRING: Robert Downey Jr. (Tony Stark/Iron Man), Gwyneth Paltrow (Pepper Potts),
Jon Favreau (Happy Hogan), Terrence Howard (James "Rhodey" Rhodes), Jeff Bridges (Obadiah Stane),
Clark Gregg (Agent Phil Coulson), Paul Bettany (voice of J.A.R.V.I.S.), Shaun Toub (Ho Yinsen),
Faran Tahir (Raza), Samuel L. Jackson (Nick Fury), Leslie Bibb (Christine Everhart)

Following a successful weapons demonstration in Afghanistan, Tony Stark is kidnapped by a terrorist group, the Ten Rings. Mortally wounded, Stark is held captive along with another prisoner, Ho Yinsen. Yinsen has managed to save Tony's life via a powerful electromagnet that keeps pieces of deadly shrapnel from entering his heart. But Tony will need a permanent solution to prevent his death.

Stark is offered his freedom in exchange for building a Jericho missile, but he knows his captors won't keep their word. With Yinsen's help, Stark builds a miniature Arc Reactor – an energy source based on his father's design – which he uses to power a suit of armor. The armored Stark breaks free, destroying the Ten Rings' weapons stockpile.

Back in the USA, he announces that Stark Industries will no longer manufacture or sell weapons. This does not sit well with Obadiah Stane, Stark's business partner. Stark creates a more powerful Arc Reactor and sleek new armor, and we learn that Stane had hired the Ten Rings to kill Stark. Stane travels to Afghanistan, meets with the Ten Rings, and steals the plans for Stark's first suit of armor.

Stane uses the plans to build a more powerful suit of armor. He attacks Stark, taking his Arc Reactor to power the new suit, and leaves Tony to die. Stark inserts his original Arc Reactor, saving his life. In his new Iron Monger armor, Stark confronts Stane, wearing his own suit. As the battle rages, Stark's assistant, Pepper Potts, overloads the enormous Arc Reactor which Howard Stark had built years ago. The power surge knocks Stane unconscious, and he falls into the Arc Reactor.

At a press conference the next day, Stark reveals to a shocked audience that he is, in fact, Iron Man.

## FIRST APPEARANCES OF:

Tony Stark, Pepper Potts, Happy Hogan, James Rhodes,
Nick Fury, Agent Coulson, Ho Yinsen, Christine Everhart,
J.A.R.V.I.S.

**01** Stane's Iron Monger armor. **02** Tony Stark shows his Arc Reactor to Obadiah Stane. **03** Iron Man takes flight.

**ROBERT DOWNEY JR., GWYNETH PALTROW, JON FAVREAU**
TONY STARK, PEPPER POTTS, HAPPY HOGAN/DIRECTOR

# The Saga Begins

The stars of *Iron Man* – the movie that started it all – reflect on ten years of Marvel Studios memories.

**W**hat was it like working together on *Iron Man*?
**Robert Downey Jr.:** Paltrow?
**Gwyneth Paltrow:** Well, these two guys, out of all the people that I've had the good fortune to work with, the triumvirate that we've formed together is very special. There's true love and real friendship over a decade.
**Jon Favreau:** We traveled around the world together. Gwyneth was my first Sherpa through Rome. And I brought my family there since then. We have really good memories. We were in Paris together with our spouses on the first trip around the world.
**RDJ:** We were in a shot-out bungalow at Hughes Aircraft off Jefferson when Jon found out that Paltrow had agreed to play Pepper Potts, and we both got really choked up for some reason because Jon said, "I know the movie's going to work now."
**GP:** Thank you!
**JF:** It's true.
**GP:** Did you really say that?
**JF:** If he says I did, he's got a better memory than I do.
**GP:** That's really nice.
**JF:** I remember we were really happy to have you on board.
**JF:** We were talking about it yesterday over dinner, Robert and I. Gwyneth is a little more…
**RDJ:** Stoic.
**JF:** She's more stoic about it, I think.

What have these ten years meant to you?
**JF:** It's nice to look at how the legacy is living on in these other movies under other filmmakers and other actors. I'm grateful that Marvel Studios have done a good job keeping it going.
**GP:** I feel like we've also lived a lot of life together. We've had babies and divorces and weddings and joys.
**RDJ:** Gwyneth told my wife to have a bunch of kids. And now we got all these kids because people listen to her.
**JF:** I remember when Apple [Gwyneth's daughter] was there for the first screen-test. Gwyneth was wearing a wig and getting dressed up in all these outfits. It was not fun. Apple walked in, and she lit up. That was the first time I really saw Gwyneth come through on camera.
**GP:** Well, remember how bad my wig looked?

**JF:** Yes.
**RDJ:** And we've been chasing that ever since!
**GP:** Wouldn't you have been in a bad mood if your wig looked like that on your screen-test?
**JF:** I wore a wig in *Iron Man* for some reason too. I wanted to wear a wig!
**RDJ:** I've avoided wigs. We don't want me in a wig. If we get to that point, we should've hung up our jerseys already.

Was there a particularly memorable moment for you on set?
**GP:** I have tons.
**RDJ:** Give us one.
**GP:** I remember on one of the movies, I broke my knee.
**JF:** Yes, I remember that.
**GP:** And Jon was like, "Okay, Blondie, let's just keep it moving!"
**RDJ:** That'd be 2. It was on *Iron Man 2*.
**JF:** No, it was on 1.
**RDJ:** On the first one, of course… someone's got to break a knee.
**GP:** We were all having dinner at this pizza place on a Saturday night. I was sitting next to Jon's wife, and my knee swelled up. She said that I had to go to see the doctor. Jon had to say he was sorry for not believing that I hurt my knee!
**JF:** Then you got X-ray'd. The doctors couldn't believe that you were able to walk!
**RDJ:** I remember doing this scene where I had a prosthetic body, and Gwyneth was reaching inside my chest. The whole scene was about Tony trusting Pepper. We rehearsed it a lot.
**JF:** That was a great one. I felt like I was coaching an improv team because I would throw in suggestions. "Okay, make it like you're playing *Operation*."
**GP:** Bzz! Ahhh!
**JF:** "Every time she reaches into your chest make like it hurts you!" And we started putting goop in there with all that slime. That was one of my favorite scenes of the whole movie.
**RDJ:** That's right. Proof that Tony Stark has a heart. We figured stuff out and then shot it. Ten years of team spirit. One, two, three… Go team! Yeah! Hoo-ha!

**04** Tony builds the Iron Man Mark II suit.

**05** Tony with the ever-loyal Happy Hogan (right).

**06** Obadiah Stane confronts Pepper Potts.

## EASTER EGGS

### A FAMILIAR THEME

Various versions of the theme from the 1966 *Iron Man* cartoon can be heard throughout the film, such as Stark's alarm call and James Rhodes' ringtone. It's also played at the Apogee Awards Ceremony, and a smooth jazz version plays at the casino.

### DRAGON AGE

As Iron Man flies down the street, a poster of the Marvel Comics alien dragon villain, Fin Fang Foom, can be seen.

### PRISONER OF THE MANDARIN?

"The Ten Rings" is the name of the group that kidnaps Stark. This villainous organization is from the comics, and is led by the Mandarin.

### CHECKMATE, STANE?

Obadiah Stane has a golden chess set in his home. This is a nod to his affiliation with the Chessmen in the comics, a group of assassins he organized to attack Stark.

### THE FIRST WHIPLASH?

A jet fighter has the callsign "Whiplash." Whiplash is the main villain of *Iron Man 2*.

### BAD BUSINESS

In the background of the final battle with Iron Monger, there's an advertisement for Roxxon Corporation. This company has been involved in a lot of the comic book storylines, including the death of Tony Stark's parents.

### KILLAH TUNES

At Tony Stark's party, the song "We Celebrate" by Ghostface Killah can be heard. Ghostface Killah has been known to use the names "Ironman" and "Tony Starks."

### THE RIVALS

Obadiah Stane plays a piano piece by the composer Antonio Salieri. Salieri was (unfairly) known for having envied his counterpart, Mozart. According to Peter Shaffer's play and movie, *Amadeus*, Salieri murdered Mozart. This parallels Stane and Stark's relationship.

### IRON MAN PAPPED!

Stark reads a newspaper which features an amateur photo of Iron Man on the cover. The image was grabbed from a video taken by a member of the public and uploaded online ahead of the film's release.

### PRESS INTRUSION

Christine Everhart, the *Vanity Fair* reporter played by Leslie Bibb, turns up in the first two *Iron Man* films. She's based on a character that appeared in the comics in 2004 (*Iron Man* Vol. 3, #75-78). At one point, Stark mistakenly addresses her as "Carrie," the title of another Stephen King novel (King also wrote *Christine*).

**07** Tony Stark tries out the repulsor technology.

**08** The Mark II armor after a vigorous testing.

**09** Suiting up for the first time in the Mark I armor.

**10** The iconic Mark III armor.

## END CREDITS SCENE

After successfully defeating Obadiah Stane and outing himself as Iron Man in a press conference, Tony Stark returns to his Malibu home only to be greeted by Nick Fury, Director of S.H.I.E.L.D. Fury reveals that Stark isn't the only Super Hero in the world: "I'm here to talk to you about the Avenger Initiative," he says.

**Significance:** Fury's plan is to create a team of formidable heroes who could defend humanity from the world's greatest threats. Today, the very idea of a Marvel Studios movie without a post-credits scene would be preposterous, but Fury's appearance and the mention of the Avengers was a hint at what was to come.

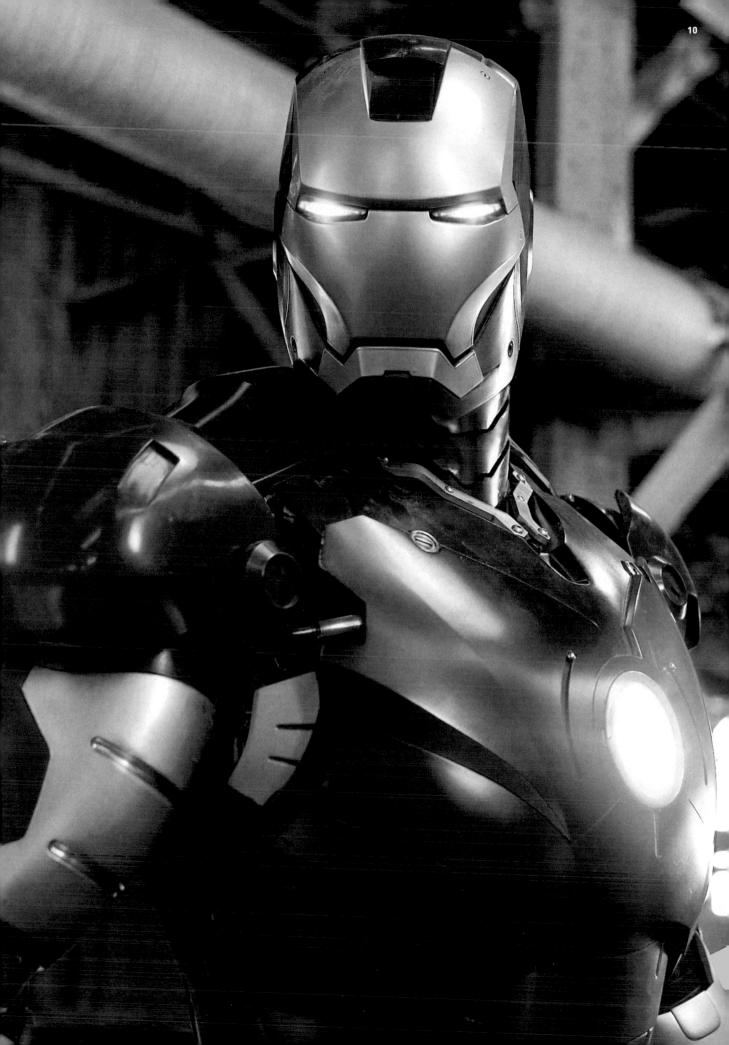

MARVEL STUDIOS

THE INCREDIBLE HULK

# THE INCREDIBLE HULK (2008)

## DIRECTED BY: LOUIS LETERRIER

STARRING: Edward Norton (Bruce Banner/Hulk), Liv Tyler (Dr Elizabeth "Betty" Ross), Tim Roth (Emil Blonsky/Abomination), William Hurt (General Thaddeus "Thunderbolt" Ross), Tim Blake Nelson (Samuel Sterns), Ty Burrell (Leonard Samson), Robert Downey Jr. (Tony Stark)

On the run from the US Army and General Ross, Bruce Banner hides out in Rocinha, Brazil. He has taught himself meditation techniques in an attempt to control his transformations, and hasn't "Hulked out" in months.

Ross discovers Banner's whereabouts, and sends a strike team led by Emil Blonsky to bring Banner back. The mission goes awry, with Banner eventually changing into his green-skinned alter ego. Hulk decimates Blonsky's team, and injures Blonsky himself before escaping

Banner makes his way back to the US, where he finds his former girlfriend, Betty Ross, working at Culver University. Meanwhile, General Ross offers Blonsky another chance to subdue Hulk. The experiment that turned Banner into Hulk was a failed attempt to duplicate the Super-Soldier Serum that created Captain America. Blonsky is given an altered version of the serum, increasing his strength.

Banner and Ross travel to New York, where they meet with scientist Samuel Sterns, who may have a cure for Banner's condition. Banner takes the cure, which reverses his transformation. He is then captured by General Ross' team.

Blonsky demands Stern give him an infusion of the serum he administered to Banner, hoping to increase his power. It works, but also transforms Blonsky into a grotesque monster. This "Abomination" rampages through New York City, hoping to draw out Hulk. General Ross agrees to let Banner fight Blonsky, and Banner leaps from a helicopter to jump-start his transformation into Hulk.

The two gamma creatures battle, leaving a trail of destruction. Hulk must also protect General Ross and his daughter Betty. Hulk defeats the Abomination, but is forced to flee from the army once more.

## FIRST APPEARANCES OF:

Bruce Banner/Hulk, Thaddeus Ross

01 Emil Blonsky, the special ops commando charged with capturing Bruce Banner. 02 The Abomination wreaks havoc in Harlem. 03 Bruce Banner's alter ego, the rage-fueled Hulk.

INTERVIEW

# WILLIAM HURT

# To Stop
# a Hulk

General Thaddeus Ross made his Marvel Studios debut in *The Incredible Hulk*, witnessing Bruce Banner's transformation. Actor William Hurt plays the military man-turned-secretary of state, nicknamed "Thunderbolt."

Thaddeus Ross made his Marvel Cinematic Universe debut in *The Incredible Hulk*. Did you enjoy playing a foil to the hero?
I did. It was amazing. I didn't have to bear the whole weight of the movie. General Ross is a perfect character to me. I felt very liberated playing him. I think all of the actors in these movies feel the same way.

There's more life in imagination and that imagination is released through the characterization. I was watching Scarlett Johansson play a scene in *Captain America: Civil War* and she was really delving into that character. She was playing that role with scalpel-like precision. She was carefully dividing Natasha Romanoff's psyche into sections.

What is the biggest challenge of appearing in a Marvel Studios movie?
Acting in film is a subtle thing. There's an 85-millimeter camera, and it can get very, very close to you. And then if the director is using a 4K camera, the audience can see every pore, whether you like it or not! I'm not the biggest fan of that. It's a really microscopic examination.

What have you enjoyed the most about this ten-year run?
I feel glad to be a participant in the whole thing. I love Marvel. Marvel stays true to itself and I'm really proud of that.

What's the secret to connecting with an audience?
The most ironic thing about art is that the more specific you get, the more universal you are. In an odd way it's a great, absurd irony that the more eccentric the idiosyncrasies, or the more idiosyncratic, the more people relate. It isn't about the millions or billions of people out there. It's about one person at a time. And that's where a lot of people who want success fail. They want to talk to lots of people rather than one person. The only way you're going to find a way to do that is by looking inside yourself, because you're the only person you can imagine being. Audiences can always relate to that because if you're being true to yourself, you're being true to them.

What's been your favorite thing about being part of the Marvel Cinematic Universe?
I have to consider the character. As an artist, it's my job to ask, "Is the character I'm playing interesting enough? Is he true enough, you know, to who we are as people? Are they believable?" That is my anchor. The really good artists pull it off.

Working on these movies has been a song for me. The Russo brothers are great guys to work with. Mike Grillo, who's the line producer for Marvel Studios, worked with me on *Body Heat*, *The Big Chill*, *The Accidental Tourist*, and *I Love You to Death*. That's over the course of 35 years, and we're still pumping. We're both still standing, anyway!

What it comes down to is the people. You have the idea, and you have the imagination. That's on the page, and they reflect great things. But, you know, in this work, we're living things. You can't just sit alone in your room with your book and have a great time. It's all about the people you are working with. That's the most important thing.

**04** General "Thunderbolt" Ross as played by acclaimed actor, William Hurt.

## EASTER EGGS

### GREEN AND BLUE
Samuel Sterns uses the name "Mr. Blue" to talk incognito to Bruce Banner. This alias was also used by Betty Ross as a way to communicate with Bruce while he was on the run in Bruce Jones' run of *Hulk* comics.

### BIRTH OF A BAD GUY
Dr. Samuel Sterns gets the Hulk's radioactive blood into his open head wound and his head begins to expand, hinting at his transformation into classic Hulk villain, the Leader.

### STARK'S ARSENAL
The Stark Industries logo is stamped on the schematics for vehicles and weaponry like the sonic cannon that the military use to attempt to subdue the Hulk.

### HULK'S ALLY
The S.H.I.E.L.D. files include a mention of Rick Jones, a character from the comic books who Bruce Banner rescued, causing Banner to turn into the Hulk for the first time.

### BRUCE'S RIVAL?
Betty's new boyfriend, Doctor Samson, is a long-standing supporting character from the comics, though he does not sport his famous green hair in the movie.

### MAKING A SUPER SOLDIER
When General Ross hands the liquid serum to Emil Blonsky, the name Dr. Reinstein is revealed. According to the *Captain America* comic books, Reinstein was the doctor who gave the Super-Soldier Serum to Steve Rogers, transforming him into Captain America.

### HIDDEN HERO
Actor Paul Soles plays Stanley, the proprietor of the pizza restaurant where Bruce is hiding. Soles provided the voice of Bruce Banner in the *Hulk* cartoon back in 1966. He was also the voice of Spider-Man in the 1967-1970 cartoon series of the same name.

### OUT OF FASHION
Betty Ross buys Bruce a pair of large purple pants. Though part of the comic iconography for Hulk, Bruce balks at the idea of wearing them.

### HULK SMASH!
Hulk rips a police car in half and uses the pieces as boxing gloves. This move was first featured in the popular video game *The Incredible Hulk: Ultimate Destruction* (2005).

### FROZEN HERO
In a deleted scene set in the Arctic (that was to be the opening to the movie), Captain America and his shield can be seen frozen in the ice.

**05** A rage in Harlem: Hulk roars at his foe.

**06** The Abomination – a creature even stronger than Hulk.

## DON'T MAKE ME ANGRY...
There are numerous references to *The Incredible Hulk* TV show (1978-1982). Culver University is a reference to the Culver Institute, where David Banner is exposed to gamma radiation. The opening titles of the film closely follow the opening titles of the TV series.

A package for Banner is addressed to "David B." This refers to the fact that Banner would have a different surname beginning with B in each episode of the TV series.

The two students who are interviewed by journalists after the fight at Culver University are called Jack McGee and Jim Wilson. Jack McGee was the name of the reporter who pursued David Banner in the classic 1970s TV series. In the comic books, Jim Wilson was the nephew of the Falcon.

Craig Armstrong, who composed the score for the film, includes the moving piano end title theme from the TV show, named "The Lonely Man" in the score.

The TV series' lead actors both make fleeting appearances. The late Bill Bixby appears on a TV screen in a scene from the movie *The Courtship of Eddie's Father*. The first live-action Hulk, Lou Ferrigno, plays a security guard and also voices Hulk.

06

## END CREDITS SCENE

General Thaddeus "Thunderbolt" Ross – partly responsible for the creation of the Abomination – drowns his sorrows in a bar, where he's approached by a smug-looking Tony Stark. "I hate to say I told you so, General," he says, "but there's a reason we put that Super-Soldier Serum on ice." "You always wear such nice suits," replies the rather curt Ross, wryly. Stark informs Ross that he's putting together a team...

**Significance:** The meeting is never again referenced, but Stark's appearance in *The Incredible Hulk* indicates that the angry green giant could be a part of the Avengers' future, and serves to show that the Marvel Cinematic Universe is interconnected.

**MARVEL** STUDIOS

# IRON MAN 2

# IRON MAN 2 (2010)

## DIRECTED BY: JON FAVREAU

STARRING: Robert Downey Jr. (Tony Stark/Iron Man), Gwyneth Paltrow (Pepper Potts), Jon Favreau (Happy Hogan), Scarlett Johansson (Natalie Rushman/Natasha Romanoff), Don Cheadle (James "Rhodey" Rhodes), Sam Rockwell (Justin Hammer), Mickey Rourke (Ivan Vanko/Whiplash), Clark Gregg (Agent Phil Coulson), Paul Bettany (voice of J.A.R.V.I.S.), John Slattery (Howard Stark), Garry Shandling (Senator Stern), Samuel L. Jackson (Nick Fury)

In Russia, a dying inventor, Anton Vanko, leaves his son Ivan with plans for the Arc Reactor. Anton had worked with Howard Stark on the original Arc Reactor years ago. With his dying words, Anton tells his son that Tony Stark's success should belong to Ivan. His father passes away, and Vanko is filled with thoughts of vengeance.

Stark learns that the palladium in his Arc Reactor is slowly poisoning him. Without a cure, and realizing that he has little time left, Stark puts Pepper Potts in charge of Stark Industries. Taking Potts's place as Stark's personal assistant is Natalie Rushman (later revealed to be S.H.I.E.L.D. agent Natasha Romanoff).

Confronted by the Senate Armed Forces Committee and Senator Stern, Stark is asked to turn over the Iron Man armor to the United States military. Stark refuses, pointing out that no other country has been able to duplicate his feat, including rival Justin Hammer.

Determined to live his life to the fullest, Stark decides to race in the Monaco Grand Prix. He is attacked by Ivan Vanko, but Stark manages to defeat him wearing a portable suit of armor. Vanko is jailed, but Hammer breaks him out, seeking his help in building a suit of armor.

Meanwhile, Stark is given a possible cure by Nick Fury and Romanoff in the form of his father's old research. Stark and his computer system J.A.R.V.I.S. synthesize a new element, update his Arc Reactor, and reverse his condition.

At the Stark Expo, Justin Hammer reveals his new drones, which are actually being controlled by Vanko. Iron Man and Rhodey, now wearing the "War Machine" armor, stop the drones, and Vanko's plans.

## FIRST APPEARANCES OF:

Natasha Romanoff (Black Widow),
Ivan Vanko (Whiplash), Justin Hammer, Peter Parker,
Senator Stern

**01** Tony Stark pushes himself to the limit as he takes part in the Monaco Grand Prix **02** Unscrupulous arms dealer, Justin Hammer.
**03** Tony and Rhodey join forces to meet the threat of Ivan Vanko.

**STAN LEE**

# The Man Behind Iron Man

The co-creator of Iron Man, Stan Lee has appeared in every Marvel Studios
movie to date, with fond memories of his time on the *Iron Man 2* set.

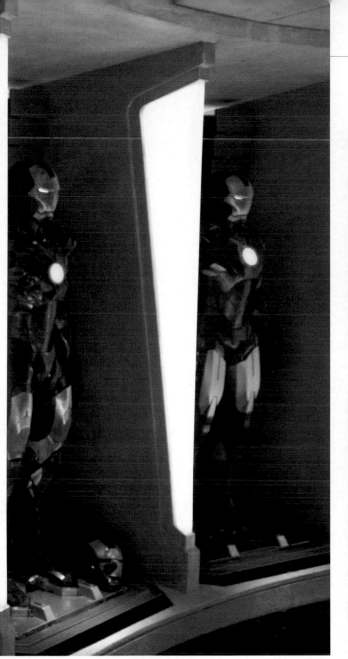

**H**ow did you feel when you saw the first *Iron Man* film?
That first movie was phenomenal. It was one of the most satisfying experiences of my life. I thought that the second movie was either its equal, or better. When I was on the set and I saw the enthusiasm on the part of the cast, and Robert Downey Jr. and Jon Favreau and everybody, I had a really good feeling about the movie.

What do you think Robert Downey Jr. brings to Tony Stark and to *Iron Man 2*?
He is so much like Tony Stark! He may not have quite as much money – though he might do if the movies keep being as successful as they are! But Robert himself is good looking, he is glamorous, he is a great guy, but he too seems to have a vulnerability about him, just like the comic book Tony Stark.

What do you think about Jon Favreau, the director?
Jon Favreau is so multitalented. He acts, he writes, he directs, and he makes everything he does seem easy. In the times I went to the set, I've never gotten a feeling of stress or crisis or urgency. He just made it all seem like it was the smoothest, easiest thing in the world. I think that feeling affected the cast and the crew, and it made everybody enjoy what they were doing and give their best.

What do you think makes *Iron Man* such a compelling character and film series?
The thing about *Iron Man* is that it's an action film. It's eye candy, but it's also a film about human beings and their relationships, and that's why people who don't normally go to these comic book-type of movies love *Iron Man*. *Iron Man* is story driven. Sure, it's got action and suspense, and all of that, but it's a story about people that we can understand, that we're interested in, that we like, and we want to see more of them.

**04** Tony Stark's Iron Man upgrades, from Mark I to IV.

**05** The legendary Stan Lee.

## EASTER EGGS

### A STERN WORD
Senator Stern, who appears in both this film and *Captain America: The Winter Soldier*, takes his name from the controversial DJ Howard Stern.

### SPIDER-BOY?
The kid wearing a toy Iron Man mask – who is rescued by Tony Stark at the expo – is a young Peter Parker...

### COVER STORY
When Tony is rummaging through his father's belongings a vintage *Captain America* comic book can be seen.

### AROUND THE WORLD
The map featuring S.H.I.E.L.D. hotspots has a number of locations highlighted, including Africa (*Black Panther*).

### STARK PROTECTS
When called to speak at the hearing before Senator Stern, Stark quips that he'd gladly accept the position of Secretary of Defense. In the 2004 comic story arc, "The Best Defense," Stark took on that role, holding the position until 2005.

### WORLD'S FAIR
Howard Stark's presentation of "The city of tomorrow" is based on Walt Disney's presentation of Epcot (Experimental Prototype Community of Tomorrow), which was planned as a city – before being turned into a theme park. Similarly, the layout of the Stark Expo is based on the 1964 New York World's Fair. The building Stark picks up when playing with the model is the Bell System Pavilion.

### FREAKS
Stark calls the government the "Freak Brothers." This refers to the underground comic characters, "the Fabulous Furry Freak Brothers."

### FRIENDS IN HIGH PLACES
The man Stark names as "The oracle of Oracle" is, in real life, the CEO of the Oracle Corporation, Larry Ellison.

### HAMMER'S MASTERPIECE
Justin Hammer states that if his "Ex-Wife" Sidewinder Self-Guided Missile was any smarter, it'd write a book that would make *Ulysses* look like it was written in crayon. When James Joyce wrote *Ulysses*, he used a red crayon, as his eyesight was failing.

10

09

11

## END CREDITS SCENE

Excusing himself from the action earlier in the film, S.H.I.E.L.D. agent Phil Coulson travels to the southwest region – more specifically, New Mexico – to deal with an issue. He reaches a crater; "Sir, we've found it," he says to Fury on the phone, as the camera reveals a giant hammer in the center of the basin. Thor's magic hammer has somehow found its way to the New Mexico desert...

**Significance:** *Iron Man 2*'s end credits scene doesn't just tease the forthcoming appearance of the God of Thunder, it also establishes Agent Coulson as an important character in uniting Earth's mightiest heroes. The scene itself is directed by Kenneth Branagh, the director of *Thor*, which was in production as *Iron Man 2* completed filming.

12

**06** Iron Man and War Machine join forces.

**07** Stark takes on Senator Stern as Rhodey looks on.

**08** S.H.I.E.L.D. agent Black Widow strikes.

**09** Tony makes a grand entrance at the Stark Expo.

**10** Iron Man soars into action as he defends himself against Vanko's arsenal.

**11** Ivan Vanko moves to take revenge against Tony Stark.

**12** Agent Coulson investigates a mysterious hammer...

# *THOR* (2011)

## DIRECTED BY: **SIR KENNETH BRANAGH**

STARRING: Chris Hemsworth (Thor), Tom Hiddleston (Loki), Anthony Hopkins (Odin), Rene Russo (Frigga), Natalie Portman (Jane Foster), Stellan Skarsgård (Erik Selvig), Kat Dennings (Darcy Lewis), Clark Gregg (Agent Coulson), Idris Elba (Heimdall), Josh Dallas (Fandral), Tadanobu Asano (Hogun), Ray Stevenson (Volstagg), Jaimie Alexander (Sif)

In Asgard, Odin is about to proclaim his son Thor as the new king. Before the ceremony is complete, a cadre of Frost Giants enter Asgard, looking to steal the Casket of Ancient Winters. They're stopped by the Destroyer, an Asgardian relic imbued with incredible power, which is nearly unstoppable. An enraged Thor seeks revenge on the Frost Giants for their audacity. With no thought of the consequences, Thor puts a daring plan into action.

Gathering his brother, Loki, and his friends Sif, Fandral, Volstagg, and Hogun, Thor travels via the Bifrost to Jotunheim, where he confronts the Frost Giants' king, Laufey. A battle ensues, which is ultimately ended by the timely arrival of Odin, who brings the Asgardians home. Angered by his son's careless actions, Odin strips Thor of his powers, banishing him to Earth until he learns humility.

While on Earth, Thor searches for his enchanted hammer, Mjolnir, and befriends astrophysicist Jane Foster. They find his hammer in a small town in New Mexico, now guarded by S.H.I.E.L.D. Thor tries to break in and retrieve the hammer, but finds he is unable to lift it – he is no longer worthy.

Loki learns that he's actually the son of Laufey, and makes a deal with the Frost Giant king to give him the Casket of Ancient Winters in exchange for killing Odin. He then sends the Destroyer to Earth, to ensure Thor cannot stop him. Deprived of his Asgardian strength, Thor nevertheless fights to save the small town and his new friends from the Destroyer's wrath. Proving himself worthy, Thor finds his powers restored. Mjølnir returns to him, and he is able to defeat the Destroyer.

Thor returns to Asgard, where he confronts Loki. The two battle on the Rainbow Bridge, with Loki falling into an abyss.

## FIRST APPEARANCES OF:

Thor, Loki, Jane Foster, Odin, Erik Selvig, Heimdall, Hogun, Volstagg, Lady Sif, Hawkeye

**01** Thor and his father, Odin, have a conflicted relationship. **02** An unworthy Thor attempts to lift Mjolnir. **03** Loki takes hold of the Casket.

INTERVIEW

## KENNETH BRANAGH

# From Asgard to Earth

Director Sir Kenneth Branagh brought a sense of Shakespearean drama to the Marvel Cinematic Universe in *Thor*. He looks back on his time in Asgard.

**What was the biggest challenge you faced during the making of *Thor*?**
The challenge was in making the marriage between the spectacular requirements of the visual and physical world of Asgard, the world of the gods, and the world of contemporary Earth. We needed to find a style that united them and allowed the characters to go from one place to the other. You get the excitement of that, you get the fish out of water, and of course, you get fun. There are characters in this universe who bring fun and loyalty and often surprise to the comics, and, I hope, to the movie as well. So trying to find that combination of the passion and the guts and the spectacle of Thor with the human dynamic is a thrill.

**Did you have a clear concept of the movie from the first day you worked on it?**
I knew the ambition was to try and combine the ancient and the modern, and that a portion of the story being on Earth was vitally important to me, so we could all understand the kinds of people they were and not live entirely in an artificial or hard-to-understand universe. In my view, the comics are full of such a rich mix, and the challenge was to combine the

elements comfortably. There are around 40 years of comics, lots of stories, 2,000 years of Norse mythology. We had to be selective, and not squash too much in. I knew which characters really interested me, so I went for those.

**Is there any specific interpretation of Thor that you were going for?**
I love them all! I love the fact that there are so many of them. I'd say we were inspired by that in the sense that I don't feel enslaved to the idea of a single look for Thor, iconic as he must be. Nevertheless, he's been iconic through many manifestations – long hair, short hair, beard, no beard, helmet with a crosspiece, square helmet, big wings, small wings, tights, trousers, armor – I'd like to think that we were able to pay a little inspiration and homage to each.

**What do you think it is about Thor that makes him stand out among Super Heroes?**
I think Thor – from the point of view of just sheer physical weight, mass, heft – is unique. As a warrior, he'd be the first in line fulfilling that cliché of never asking anybody else to do what he wouldn't do himself. In fact, half the time you've got to try and stop him from doing it!

**04** Jaimie Alexander (Sif) and Branagh talk through a scene. **05** Kenneth Branagh behind the camera on the Asgard set.

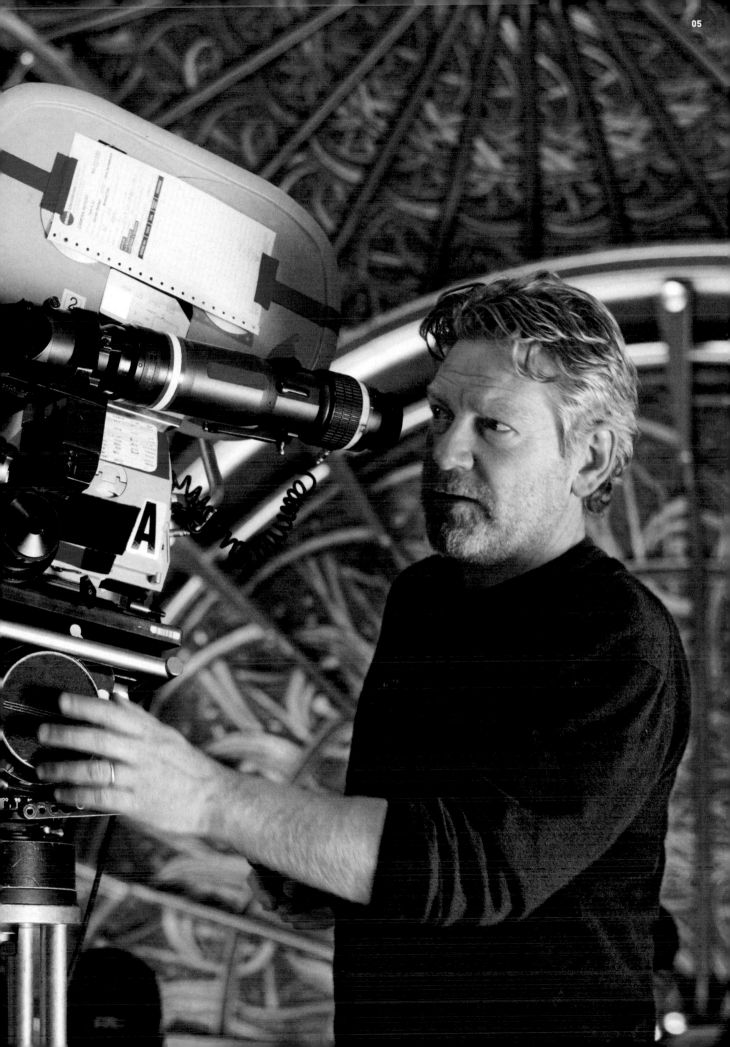

## EASTER EGGS

### MJOLNIR IN THE STONE
Stan Lee's cameo (in the truck trying to pull Mjolnir out of the ground) might be obvious, but the bearded trucker who first tries to release the hammer is in fact J. Michael Straczynski, creator of *Babylon 5* and writer of a popular *Thor* run which began in 2007.

### STRANGE THINGS
There are several artifacts in the Asgardian vault, one of which is the Orb of Agamotto. In the comics, the Orb is a powerful scrying ball which can help locate magic use across the globe, often used by Doctor Strange.

### BILLBOARD COMICS
A tourist billboard advertises New Mexico as "Land of Enchantment – Journey into Mystery," which is a reference to the comic book series *Journey into Mystery*.

### DR. ALIAS
In the original run of *Thor*, the mighty god was sent down to Earth and into the body of disabled med-student, Donald Blake. The alias has popped up over the years and is winked at with Thor's fake ID.

### HAWKEYE IN THE SKY
Well before the Avengers had assembled, a lone S.H.I.E.L.D. archer is dispatched to take down the depowered God of Thunder.

### FIRST GLIMPSE
In the Asgardian weapons vault, the Infinity Gauntlet can be seen briefly against a far wall. The gauntlet houses the Infinity Stones that have popped up in virtually every Marvel film. It's later dismissed in *Thor: Ragnarok* as being a fake.

### THE WRITE PART
During the banquet at the end of *Thor*, the prolific *Thor* comics writer and artist Walt Simonson is seated directly next to Sif.

**06** Thor kneels before Odin, in a rare moment of humility.

**07** Heimdall opens the Bifrost bridge.

**08** Loki dons his distinctive headpiece.

**09** Chris Hemsworth and Tom Hiddleston go before the cameras.

## END CREDITS SCENE

Nick Fury – impressed with Selvig's work in the New Mexico situation – meets with the astrophysicist in a S.H.I.E.L.D. facility. Describing the events of *Thor* as "unprecedented," Selvig is surprised when Fury opens a briefcase to reveal a glowing blue cube: the Tesseract, an otherworldly object of potentially unlimited power. Looking at Selvig's reflection, Loki appears and is in control of Selvig. "Well, I guess that's worth a look," whispers the God of Mischief, which Selvig repeats.

**Significance:** While the Tesseract could be mistaken for a throwaway MacGuffin, it is actually the first appearance of one of the six Infinity Stones, which become integral to the overarching narrative of the Marvel Cinematic Universe. It isn't long before we become reacquainted with the Tesseract, as it appears next in *Captain America: The First Avenger.*

# CAPTAIN AMERICA: THE FIRST AVENGER (2011)

## DIRECTED BY: JOE JOHNSTON

STARRING: Chris Evans (Steve Rogers/Captain America), Hayley Atwell (Peggy Carter), Sebastian Stan (James Buchanan "Bucky" Barnes), Tommy Lee Jones (Colonel Chester Phillips), Stanley Tucci (Dr. Abraham Erskine), Dominic Cooper (Howard Stark), Hugo Weaving (Johann Schmidt/Red Skull), Toby Jones (Dr. Arnim Zola), Samuel L. Jackson (Nick Fury)

During the dark days of World War II, Johann Schmidt – known more infamously as the Red Skull – and his Hydra soldiers race to obtain the Tesseract, an artifact of incredible power. Schmidt plans on tapping into its energies to create terrifying weapons with which to bring the Allied Forces to their knees, and conquer the world.

Back in the US, frail Steve Rogers attempts to enlist in the Army. Denied entry due to his physical weaknesses, Rogers is nevertheless selected by Dr. Abraham Erskine to participate in Project Rebirth. Chosen for his selflessness and innate humanity, Rogers receives the Super-Soldier Serum, which transforms him into a specimen of peak human perfection. Erskine is assassinated by a Nazi spy, leaving Rogers as the only Super Soldier.

Codenamed "Captain America," Rogers partakes in public relations stunts designed to boost morale in the war effort. Rogers yearns to use his newfound abilities to help the Allied soldiers fighting in Europe, and stop the Red Skull. When his childhood friend, James Barnes, is captured along with the rest of his unit, Rogers stages a daring raid to free everyone. From that moment on, Rogers is an active combatant, a symbol of hope and freedom.

Attacking the Red Skull's stronghold, Rogers makes his way aboard the Hydra leader's now airborne Valkyrie bomber. He manages to stop the Skull, but cannot disarm the weapons the bomber carries, which will lay waste to much of the Eastern United States. In a last-ditch effort, Rogers crashes the plane into the icy ocean below. Nearly 70 years later, a frozen Rogers is discovered and revived. He meets Nick Fury, who asks him to join the Avengers...

## FIRST APPEARANCES OF:

Steve Rogers, Peggy Carter, Young Howard Stark,
Red Skull, Dr. Arnim Zola, Bucky Barnes,
the Howling Commandos

**01** Steve Rogers prior to his involvement in a life-changing experiment. **02** Doctor Abraham Erskine demonstrates his amazing formula. **03** Captain America races into action.

## CHRIS EVANS

# Super Soldier and Super Hero

Actor Chris Evans looks back on facing his fears and making his debut as the iconic Marvel Super Hero, Captain America.

**W**hat appeals to you the most about playing Captain America?
Steve Rogers is a man who wants very much to do good and serve his country in World War II, but he's been rejected from the Army for having asthma and other health challenges. Because of his good values and morals, Steve is chosen by a man named Dr. Erskine for an experiment to create a "Super Soldier." He is injected with a serum that turns him into Captain America – and Dr. Erskine knows Steve won't take advantage of the gift of power and will always protect the weak.

How much did you know about Captain America before making *The First Avenger*?
My first exposure to the character was probably a video game my buddy had, and Captain America was one of the characters.

How did you feel taking on the role?
At first, I was scared and nervous. It's something a lot of fans care about, so you just want to make sure you do it justice. But I don't think you should live your life based on fear, so I went for it.

When you agreed to the role, did you go back and look through the comics?
I did read a lot of comic books for basic things like how he throws his shield, how he runs – things like that.

How were the film's different looks for Steve Rogers achieved?
Well, there's skinny Steve – or "early Steve," as we called

him. Early Steve is obviously before the transformation. That's all special effects – they did a good job of taking my body and just shrinking me down. Then, when he becomes Captain America, there are a couple of different scenes. Initially, he's put in this very silly Captain America costume. And I have a sidekick in the film called Bucky, who gets captured, and there's a big sequence where I rescue him, so there's the "Bucky rescue outfit," as everyone calls it. And then the Captain America suit, the big finale suit. That went through a lot of different designs, and I think it looks fantastic.

04 Steve checks out what will become Captain America's shield. 05 The inspirational Captain America.

## EASTER EGGS

### FRIENDS LIKE THESE

The team who support Captain America are known as the Howling Commandos. In the comics, they were led by Nick Fury, and included members Gabe Jones and Dum Dum Dugan. Two members, Bucky Barnes and James Montgomery Falsworth (a.k.a. Union Jack), were part of the World War II super-powered team the Invaders, led by Captain America.

### GOOD THINGS COME IN TREES

The World Tree (or Yggdrasill) from Norse mythology is seen on an ancient chamber behind the Red Skull. It would later be drawn by Thor to show Jane Foster the concept of the Nine Realms.

### PASSING THE TORCH

At the Stark Expo, we see an android in a red jumpsuit, kept beneath a glass dome. This is the original Human Torch, Marvel's first Super Hero, who debuted in 1939 while the company was known as Timely Comics. The Torch was later a member of the Invaders, and Johnny Storm adopted the name as a member of the Fantastic Four. Chris Evans played the latter role in two films.

### STAN-D IN

Although Captain America was created by Joe Simon and Jack Kirby, Stan Lee was responsible for reviving the character as a member of the Avengers in 1964.

### LOOKING TO THE FUTURE

Just prior to Bucky's fall, he picks up Cap's shield and uses it to protect himself – a reference to the character's role in the comics as the replacement Captain America, when Steve Rogers is thought dead.

### HEAD IN THE RIGHT DIRECTION

Our first shot of Arnim Zola is through a huge magnifying glass, giving him close to the appearance he has in the comics (a giant head projected onto a screen). The schematics of this very look are on the table next to him. Later, in *The Winter Soldier*, we actually see Zola's bizarre form come to fruition.

### CAP VS. HITLER

The Captain America stage show Steve Rogers performs includes a section where he punches out Hitler, which re-creates the famous scene from the cover of *Captain America Comics* #1.

**06** The Howling Commandos join Bucky Barnes on the battlefield.

**07** The sinister Red Skull.

**08** S.H.I.E.L.D. founder member, Peggy Carter.

**09** Howard Stark, the man who created Captain America's shield.

**10** Nick Fury enlists Steve Rogers into the Avengers Initiative.

## END CREDITS SCENE

After Steve Rogers' plane nosedives into the ocean (with the Tesseract onboard), he wakes up in the modern day. Cut to an empty gym – a brusque Cap is pounding the life out of a punchbag, sending it careering across the room. He's a man out of time: his friends, his sweetheart, and his mission all behind him. "Trying to get me back in the world?" he asks an approaching Fury. "Trying to save it," Fury replies.

What follows is a kinetic montage featuring short clips from *The Avengers*. Taken from the Joss Whedon-directed film, the "scene" acts as a teaser trailer for the upcoming film.

MARVEL STUDIOS

THE AVENGERS

# THE AVENGERS (2012)

## DIRECTED BY: JOSS WHEDON

STARRING: Robert Downey Jr. (Tony Stark/Iron Man), Chris Evans (Steve Rogers/Captain America), Chris Hemsworth (Thor), Scarlett Johansson (Natasha Romanoff/Black Widow), Mark Ruffalo (Bruce Banner/Hulk), Jeremy Renner (Clint Barton/Hawkeye), Clark Gregg (Agent Phil Coulson), Samuel L. Jackson (Nick Fury), Cobie Smulders (Agent Maria Hill), Stellan Skårsgard (Erik Selvig), Tom Hiddleston (Loki), Paul Bettany (voice of J.A.R.V.I.S.)

While researching the Tesseract at a secret S.H.I.E.L.D. facility, scientist Erik Selvig and S.H.I.E.L.D. agent Clint Barton are brought under the control of Loki. The God of Mischief steals the Tesseract, which he plans to trade to an unknown being of immense power, in exchange for an alien army he can use to conquer Earth.

Nick Fury realizes what's at stake, and sends Natasha Romanoff to locate Bruce Banner, and Agent Phil Coulson to enlist the help of Tony Stark. The two scientists are tasked with locating the Tesseract, and Fury brings in Captain America to help recover it. They come into conflict with Loki in a battle soon joined by Thor and Iron Man. Loki is captured, and brought aboard the S.H.I.E.L.D. helicarrier.

Refusing to reveal the location of the Tesseract, Loki subtly manipulates the heroes, until Banner eventually transforms into Hulk, wreaking havoc. Loki escapes, and prepares to summon his invading army. The team of heroes, calling themselves the Avengers, gathers in New York City to stop them.

The Battle of New York rages, and the Chitauri invaders do their best to lay waste to the city. The Avengers stop them at every turn, but unless they can close a portal Loki has opened above Stark Tower, the aliens will continue to stream through, threatening Earth. The World Security Council orders a nuclear strike on New York.

Faced with the double jeopardy of alien invasion on one hand and nuclear armageddon on the other, the Avengers rise to the challenge. While Black Widow, Hawkeye, Captain America, Thor, and Hulk stand fast against the Chitauri armada, Iron Man races against time to intercept the missile. The armored Avenger succeeds, grabbing the missile and directing it through the portal to the Chitauri homeworld. Romanoff closes the portal, and New York is saved.

## FIRST APPEARANCES OF:

Maria Hill, Thanos

01 S.H.I.E.L.D. agents Maria Hill and Phil Coulson. 02 Captain America defends New York from an alien onslaught. 03 Loki lords it over humanity.

**JEREMY RENNER**

# Taking Aim

After making a cameo/uncredited appearance as a S.H.I.E.L.D. agent in *Thor*, Clint Barton alias actor Jeremy Renner make their proper debut as Super Hero archer Hawkeye in *The Avengers*!

Is there a sense of responsibility when you play a Super Hero? What was it like working with the other franchises?
I'm not a guy that says, "I'm a role model," but I see that there is a sense of responsibility that comes with playing this kind of character. That is very important to me. It's a reflection of all of our hard work on these films.

Is it important that these films are still story and character based?
Yes, I think that's part of the secret sauce that Marvel has. It's not just about slinging arrows and flying with hammers and that kind of thing. It makes fun of itself when it needs to. It's serious when it needs to be serious. It's grounded, and then it's a huge spectacle and ridiculous and action packed. And then there is that sense of humor which I think is one of the best ingredients in this kind of storytelling.

Do you remember your initial reaction to the first *Iron Man* movie?
Absolutely. I was a huge fan. I've always been a huge fan of Robert Downey Jr. – and that was what got me sold on the idea of what Marvel Studios were doing from the very first film. They made it really plausible. I really believed in the world of Iron Man, with all the tech.

Do you enjoy crossing over with other franchises?
Yes. In *Captain America: Civil War*, that happened a lot in the big battle in the airport. I had to keep check on what my relationship was to the other characters. So I had to keep some truth to it. I think for fans it's pretty epic.
As a fan myself, it doesn't really get more exciting than to have that many Super Heroes and that many talented actors who are just wonderful people to work with.
It's always a blast. There's always something fresh and new to do. I think that's what's exciting for fans and exciting for us. You just don't know what to expect. Marvel have really good ideas for the storytelling frameworks and all those characters within it. They've come up with a really wonderful model.

What are your fondest memories of playing Hawkeye?
I remember going to a meeting with Kevin Feige to talk about Clint Barton. The role was really interesting to me because he was a really easy character to relate to. He's a guy that doesn't have any kind of super power. I was asked to do a quick little introduction to Hawkeye in that first *Thor* movie. My questions to Kevin were, "How are you going to do the *Thor* movie? How are you going to get this Fabio lookalike handsome guy flying with a hammer? How do you make it intergalactic yet also grounded?" And they did it! With the right directors and the right writing it just works. Chris Hemsworth can just pull that off like nobody else's business.
It's been an amazing journey, but it was tough to establish Hawkeye's character early on because there are no movies devoted to the character and in the first *Avengers* movie he was hypnotized. But it's been a really wonderful 10-year journey – or not even 10 years, because I didn't start until 2011. It doesn't seem like it's that long. The relationships that we've established are what feel long. That's what feels like an eternity in a really great way. The bond of the Avengers essentially is really strong on camera and off camera.

**04** Jeremy Renner as Hawkeye.

## EASTER EGGS

### NOT WHO HE SEEMS?

Stark attempts to evade Agent Phil Coulson's phone call by claiming to be a Life Model Decoy. The term refers to androids designed by S.H.I.E.L.D. that function as decoys.

### DRAGON AGE

During Loki's raid on the S.H.I.E.L.D. facility, a sign can be seen indicating that its codename is "Project Pegasus." In the Marvel comics, Project Pegasus is an acronym for "Potential Energy Group/Alternate Sources/United States," an organization which researches alternative fuels. Their top-secret work involves using super-powered individuals in their experiments. Project Pegasus was the base for the Squadron Supreme and was used as a prison for super-powered enemies or dangerous objects that could not otherwise be contained.

### BIRDS OF A FEATHER

Two ravens can be spotted when Thor first confronts Loki, a nod to Odin's pet watchmen, Huginn and Muninn.

### FEELING HUNGRY?

During the climactic final battle, Iron Man lands next to a shawarma restaurant, which would later serve as the location in one of the end credits scenes.

### TIME TO REBUILD

After the destruction at the end of the movie, Tony looks over the blueprints for Avengers Tower. The plans include symbols for each member's quarters shown by their icons: Thor's hammer, Captain America's shield, etc.

### A TAGLINE FIT FOR HEROES

In his conversation with Loki, Stark refers to the Avengers as "Earth's mightiest heroes." This is the longstanding tagline of the comic, and was the subtitle of the *Avengers* animated series that ran from 2010 - 2012.

### COULSON'S CARDS

The iconic *Captain America #1* cover features on one of Agent Coulson's prized trading cards.

### INCREDIBLE!

The various grunts, groans, and iconic lines issued by Hulk are voiced by Lou Ferrigno, the star of the 1970s *The Incredible Hulk* TV series.

### IRON MAN PAPPED!

The fighter jet which Hulk smashes is the same prop jet used in the movie *True Lies*. The U.S. military lends its hardware to movie shoots if there's a U.S. military presence in the film. As *The Avengers* only features the fictional S.H.I.E.L.D. and non-military emergency services, the production team had to buy a jet.

05

06

07

08

09

10

## END CREDITS SCENES

*The Avengers* was the first Marvel Studios film to feature two credits scenes.

In the mid-credits scene, we learn that Loki is not acting alone. The Other informs his master that Earth is not so easily overwhelmed. "They are unruly and therefore cannot be ruled. To challenge them is to court Death," he proclaims, as his master rises and grins menacingly, revealing the puppet master: Thanos, the Mad Titan.

The credits end with a light-hearted scene echoing back to Iron Man's earlier line where he insists the team go out for shawarma. Interestingly, this scene was shot by Joss Whedon on the night of the film's world premiere – if you look closely, Captain America covers his face as he eats because the actor, Chris Evans, is sporting a beard.

**Significance:** The Other's mention of Death alludes to Thanos' obsession with trying to impress the personification of Death in the comics...

**05** Loki takes on Captain America.

**06** The Chitauri invade.

**07** Thor attempts to stop Hulk's rampage.

**08** Clint and Natasha share a quiet moment.

**09** Iron Man repels the alien invaders.

**10** An enraged Hulk strikes

# *IRON MAN 3* (2013)

## DIRECTED BY: **SHANE BLACK**

STARRING: Robert Downey Jr. (Tony Stark/Iron Man), Gwyneth Paltrow (Pepper Potts),
Jon Favreau (Happy Hogan), Don Cheadle (James "Rhodey" Rhodes), Paul Bettany (voice of J.A.R.V.I.S.),
Guy Pearce (Aldrich Killian), Rebecca Hall (Maya Hansen), Ben Kingsley (Trevor Slattery/the Mandarin),
William Sadler (President Ellis), Miguel Ferrer (Vice President Rodriguez), Ty Simpkins (Harley Keener)

Following the Battle of New York, Tony Stark has become obsessed with building Iron Man armor, creating a literal cocoon around himself. This drives a wedge between Tony and Pepper Potts, who has been asked by Aldrich Killian to join his company, Advanced Idea Mechanics. Years ago, Killian had tried to interest Stark in the work of his then-new company. Stark brushed off the eager young entrepreneur, and a rivalry was born.

A new threat arises in the form of the Mandarin, a terrorist striking at the U.S. The attacks hit Stark hard when Happy Hogan is caught in one of the Mandarin's assaults. Stark issues a challenge to the Mandarin on live TV, inviting the terrorist to meet him at Stark's Malibu home. The Mandarin obliges, and Stark's home is destroyed, along with Stark (apparently).

In reality, Stark's Iron Man armor has flown him to Tennessee to lay low. His armor damaged, Stark is forced to rely on his wits and intelligence, along with the help of a young science enthusiast named Harley. He learns that the Mandarin is using enhanced soldiers as his weapons, men and women who have undergone the Extremis process.

Stark tracks the Mandarin to Miami, where he learns the Mandarin is just an actor named Trevor Slattery working for Killian. Killian plans to kill the U.S. president, so that the vice president (already under his control) can assume power. Killian would then hold sway over the president and the Mandarin, controlling global events for profit.

Stark leads an assault on Killian's stronghold, using J.A.R.V.I.S to control all his suits of Iron Man armor. He ultimately stops Killian. Realizing that he can no longer shut himself off from the world, Stark has the shrapnel near his heart removed, along with the Arc Reactor.

## FIRST APPEARANCES OF:

The Mandarin, Aldrich Killian, Harley Keener

**01** Tony and Pepper take their relationship to the next level. **02** The Mandarin's attack gets a little too close to home. **03** Stark's Iron Man armor meets a new friend.

INTERVIEW

## DON CHEADLE

# A Friend of Iron

With an extra pair of Iron shoes to fill, Don Cheadle steps in as Iron Man's right-hand man and loyal friend, James "Rhodey" Rhodes alias War Machine.

**W**hat did you think when you saw the Iron Patriot suit for the first time?
I thought, "Wow, that thing looks heavy!" (*laughs*) And I wasn't wrong! It's great to see these different iterations of who this War Machine guy is, and really sort of fundamentally address who the guy is inside of the armor and how does he tick? That's really what we're trying to get into the meat of.

**The suit is heavy, and you have to wear it when it's 100 degrees out. Does that ever get to you?**
It's one of those things where you go, "Oh wow, I get to be War Machine, I get to be Iron Patriot, I get to wear all of that," and then you start putting it on and 30 minutes later as they're still screwing you into this thing, you're like, "I signed up for this?" But look, we get to play make-believe with the best toys. And even

when I've seen some stuff just roughly cut together, the things I saw at Comic-Con and the things on the set, it's exciting!

**What is it about the Marvel Studios movies that makes them always seem to hit their mark with the audience?**
I think the way that Marvel is able to intricately weave these storylines and have people show up in each other's storylines, and how after each film there's a departure point where the next storyline could come in... they're just smart! There's an excitement that gets generated for the next myth, and how is it going to be told. And I also think there's a real sense of humor about it, so it's not taken too seriously.

**Will War Machine be appearing in any other films?**
Let's start that happening! Let's get that going. I mean, I should've been in *The Avengers*!

**04** Rhodey dons the Iron Patriot armor. **05** Don Cheadle as James "Rhodey" Rhodes

## EASTER EGGS

In the comics, Killian's organization, A.I.M. (Advanced Idea Mechanics) is an offshoot of Hydra. Since Hydra was still in the shadows at this stage, it's possible Killian was part of it.

### PRESIDENTIAL WRITER

President Ellis is named for Warren Ellis, the writer of the original "Extremis" storyline that was adapted into this movie.

### CAPTAIN ANARCHY

When the fake Mandarin removes his hood, a tattoo of Captain America's shield is revealed. However, this one has an "A" in the center that stands for "anarchy"!

### IN FRONT OF AND BEHIND THE CAMERA

When Tony Stark signs an autograph for two kids, he tells one of them that he looks like Ralphie Parker from the 1983 movie *A Christmas Story*. The actor who played Ralphie, Peter Billingsley, was a producer on the first two *Iron Man* films.

### WALK OF FAME

When the Extremis-infected soldier kneels down outside Grauman's Chinese Theatre, the actor's actual handprints can be seen in the cement.

### EPIC A.I.M.

Some of the scenes shot outside the A.I.M. headquarters were filmed at Epic Games in North Carolina. Epic have developed the innovative Unreal engine, plus several video games, including *Gears of War* and *Fortnite*.

### OLD FRIENDS

In the opening flashback we meet Doctor Yinsen, the man who helped Tony build his first suit in the cave. The good doctor even references this initial meeting to Tony in the first movie.

06

07

08

09

## END CREDITS SCENE

Tony Stark lies on a therapist's couch, sharing his most intimate thoughts and experiences. The camera pulls round to reveal Bruce Banner as the "therapist," napping in his chair. "I'm sorry, I'm not that kind of doctor… I don't have that kind of… temperament," says Banner, leading Stark to rewind to his teenage years and recount where it all started going wrong.

**Significance:** This scene shows how Stark and Banner have remained peers following the incident in New York. As two of the Marvel Cinematic Universe's top intellectuals, it's no surprise they remain close.

**06** Pepper Potts gets in on the action.

**07** Down but not out, Tony Stark relies on his wits to defeat Aldrich Killian.

**08** Killian, the power behind the Mandarin.

**09** Tony Stark – defeated?

**10** The Mark 42 armored suit.

**11** The Mandarin's attack on Stark gets too close to home.

# THOR: THE DARK WORLD (2013)

## DIRECTED BY: ALAN TAYLOR

STARRING: Chris Hemsworth (Thor), Tom Hiddleston (Loki), Anthony Hopkins (Odin), Rene Russo (Frigga), Natalie Portman (Jane Foster), Stellan Skarsgård (Erik Selvig), Kat Dennings (Darcy Lewis), Idris Elba (Heimdall), Zachary Levi (Fandral), Tadanobu Asano (Hogun), Ray Stevenson (Volstagg), Jaimie Alexander (Sif), Christopher Eccleston (Malekith), Adewale Akinnuoye-Agbaje (Algrim/Kurse)

After the Avengers' battle in New York, Loki is brought before Odin. The All-Father punishes Loki and orders him imprisoned. Thor and his companions Sif, Fandral, Hogun, and Volstagg, wage war in Vanaheim against invading marauders, and emerge victorious. When Thor returns to Asgard, he checks in with Heimdall, who has been keeping an eye on Jane Foster for him.

On Earth, Jane Foster investigates a strange phenomenon, and is transported to another world. There, she encounters a substance that infests her body – the Aether. Foster reappears as Thor arrives on Earth, and they travel to Asgard to check on Jane's condition. Incensed that his son has brought a human to Asgard, Odin demands that Thor return Jane to Earth. As a guard touches her wrist, the Aether protects Jane, and Odin agrees to find a way to remove it.

Alerted to the awakening of the Aether, the Dark Elves are determined to take it back – with it, they can destroy the Nine Realms. Under their leader Malekith, they attack Asgard. Frigga fights Malekith to protect Foster, but is killed. Thor drives off Malekith, and a grief-stricken Odin imprisons Foster.

Thor breaks Foster out of prison, along with Loki, and the three travel to the world of Svartalfheim. Drawn to the Aether, Malekith and the Dark Elves attempt to seize it once more. Malekith succeeds, while Loki appears to sacrifice himself to save Thor and Foster. The two find a portal, and travel back to Earth.

Malekith plans to use the Aether to destroy the Nine Realms. Thor defeats him, and Foster sends Malekith back to Svartalfheim. When Thor returns to Asgard, he tells Odin that he's not yet ready to be his successor, and departs. Unknown to Thor, "Odin" is really Loki, who has assumed power in Asgard.

## FIRST APPEARANCE OF:

The Collector

**01** Thor takes on marauders on the battlefeld. **02** Malekith, the ancient leader of the Dark Elves **03** Jane Foster finds herself under threat from the mysterious powers of the Aether.

INTERVIEW

INTERVIEW

**CHRIS HEMSWORTH**

# Whosoever Holds This Hammer

Much like Thor himself, Chris Hemsworth has proved to be a worthy wielder of Mjolnir. Here, he looks back on his second outing as the God of Thunder.

04

This was your third time picking up the hammer to play Thor. What was it like to revisit the character?

I love playing him. The trick is to find new ways each time to make the character have some sort of advance or growth from the last one, and not repeat things you've already done. And that's a part of the job of the director, writer, and the actors all coming together and saying, "What's the next step?"

What was it like working with Anthony Hopkins and building on the relationship you established in the first film?

It was great. We were at different stages of our own lives, much like the characters we played in the movie. I was certainly a little more comfortable in the skin of this character. Anthony felt like I'd matured, therefore that Thor has matured, and as a result, Odin spoke to him differently, and vice versa.

How did the relationship between Thor and Loki change throughout all the movies?

At the beginning of the first film, they were brothers and there was less hatred involved. In *The Avengers*, it was just us kind of yelling at each other and butting heads, but in *Thor: The Dark World*, we arrived at a place where their relationship is more like it was in the first film. They still clashed in *Thor: The Dark World*, but for the most part, I think it made for a far more interesting dynamic.

When you read the screenplay for *Thor: The Dark World*, what did you connect with most in terms of fleshing out the character?

When I read a script, I'm always looking for some sort of conflict. I try to discover what it is that Thor is trying to work through, as opposed to him just being there and being central to the situation.

**04** Thor enjoys a more equal relationship with his father, Odin. **05** The God of Thunder faces a threat from the distant past.

06

**06** Lady Sif leads
the charge!

**07** Jane Foster and
Frigga prepare to defend
themselves against the
Dark Elves' attack.

**08** Jane and Loki are
uneasy allies as the
battle intensifies.

**09** The sinister Dark
Elves take control.

**10** Kurse, the brutal
lieutenant of
Malekith's army.

**11** Thor stands watch
over Asgard.

**12** Malekith, leader of
the Dark Elves.

07

08

09

## END CREDITS SCENES

Asgardians Sif and Volstagg journey to meet Taneleer Tivan, otherwise known as the Collector, an Elder of the Universe who has amassed an incredible collection of artifacts and creatures from around the cosmos. They are there to deliver the Aether. Sif and Volstagg reveal that the Aether is another of the Infinity Stones, and that keeping it in Asgard's vaults alongside the Tesseract would not be wise (when collected, all six Stones can be wielded with infinite power). After the Asgardians leave, the Collector mutters, "One down, five to go."

**Significance:** The scene – directed by *Guardians of the Galaxy*'s James Gunn – is our first glimpse into the Guardians world, where the Collector features in a larger role, and confirms that the Aether and Tesseract are both Infinity Stones, building on the larger plot of the Marvel Cinematic Universe's first three phases.

## EASTER EGGS

### WORLD ON FIRE

When Thor and Malekith fight across the realms, a number of the Nine Worlds are represented. One particular world is Muspelheim, the burning home of Thor's most deadly foe, the Fire Giant Surtur, who later faces the God of Thunder in *Thor Ragnarok*.

### HIS OLDEST FOE

The giant rock warrior that Thor smashes into pieces during the opening battle is a Kronan. The Kronans fought Thor in his first ever appearance, *Journey into Mystery* #83, and appeared in *Guardians of the Galaxy Vol. 2* and *Thor: Ragnarok*.

### HARD SCIENCE

Erik Selvig's chalkboard references the "616 Universe," "The Fault," and "The Crossroads." The "616 Universe" is the designation for the main Marvel Universe in the comic books. "The Fault" first appeared in *War of Kings* #6. It is a tear in the universe that is a path to a number of alternate realities. "The Crossroads" in the comic books is a weird alternative reality that Doctor Strange dispatches a rampaging Hulk to in an effort to protect the Earth.

**MARVEL STUDIOS**

# CAPTAIN AMERICA
## THE WINTER SOLDIER

# CAPTAIN AMERICA: THE WINTER SOLDIER (2014)

## DIRECTED BY: ANTHONY RUSSO, JOE RUSSO

STARRING: Chris Evans (Steve Rogers/Captain America), Samuel L. Jackson (Nick Fury), Scarlett Johansson (Natasha Romanoff/Black Widow), Anthony Mackie (Sam Wilson/Falcon), Sebastian Stan (James Buchanan "Bucky" Barnes/ Winter Soldier), Robert Redford (Alexander Pierce), Cobie Smulders (Maria Hill), Frank Grillo (Brock Rumlow), Emily VanCamp (Sharon Carter/Agent 13), Toby Jones (Dr Arnim Zola), Jenny Agutter (Councilwoman Hawley)

Steve Rogers is trying to adjust to life in the modern world as well as continuing to work with Nick Fury and Natasha Romanoff as a S.H.I.EL.D. operative. While on a morning run, he meets Sam Wilson, a fellow veteran. The two bond, as Romanoff arrives to take Rogers on a new mission.

That mission ultimately results in Romanoff following her own secret mission from Fury. After obtaining top-secret S.H.I.E.L.D. intelligence on a thumb drive, Rogers is angry with Fury's misinformation. To mollify Rogers, Fury shows him Project Insight – a series of three next gen Helicarriers designed to eliminate enemy threats. Fury tries to access the data on the thumb drive, but finds he doesn't have clearance. He confronts his superior, Alexander Pierce, and requests that Project Insight be delayed. Following an aborted attempt by the S.H.I.E.L.D. strike team to bring him into custody, Rogers escapes from S.H.I.E.L.D.'s headquarters, the Triskelion.

Fury is attacked en route to Maria Hill, but escapes to Rogers' apartment. He gives Rogers the thumb drive, and tells him to trust no one. He is then shot several times by a masked assassin. Rogers gives chase and throws his shield at the assailant, who catches the shield with a cybernetic arm and throws it back as he escapes.

With Romanoff's help, Rogers learns that S.H.I.E.L.D. has been compromised by Hydra, and that Pierce is in charge. The organization plans to use Project Insight to eliminate any threats to them – including heroes like Tony Stark and Bruce Banner. Aided by Romanoff, Wilson, and Fury, Rogers stops Pierce's plans, disabling the three Helicarriers. Rogers confronts the mysterious assailant, known as the Winter Soldier, who is revealed to be his old friend, James "Bucky" Barnes.

## FIRST APPEARANCES OF:

Sharon Carter, Sam Wilson, Brock Rumlow, Alexander Pierce, Wolfgang von Strucker, Wanda and Pietro Maximoff

01 Sam Wilson meets Steve Rogers on a morning run. 02 Barnes takes pause in his mission. 03 Nick Fury, director of S.H.I.E.L.D.

INTERVIEW

## ANTHONY & JOE RUSSO

# The Heroes' War

The directing brothers who have overseen four Marvel movies began their Marvel Studios career with *Captain America: The Winter Soldier*, a movie that set the standard for what was to come.

**W**hat do you like so much about Captain America as a character?

**Anthony Russo:** He's such a great character! He hasn't been corrupted or compromised.

**Joe Russo:** You're plucking a guy out of the greatest generation and slamming him into this cultural mess. Some of the best lines in the movie have to do with Cap's point of view about that. He has real conflict – Cap came from a different generation. He is loyal to the government, and to the United States, but with S.H.I.E.L.D., it deals with gray areas.

Black Widow is a pretty gray character. What was the thinking behind teaming her with Captain America?

**JR:** That's exactly why she fits so well.

**AR:** We couldn't resist putting those two characters together. Cap has such a strong moral code and Black Widow lies for a living – they are like fire and water.

Why did you want to use the Winter Soldier story arc?

**JR:** The greatest thing as a director from a storytelling standpoint is to have that strong emotional connection between the hero and the villain.

**AR:** Captain America is so morally strong – how do you shake someone like that? You have to throw something at them as complex as the Winter Soldier to really threaten them.

In the comic books, the Winter Soldier has quite an emotional journey. Did you keep that in mind when you introduced him?

**JR:** We were mindful that there would be future movies, and this character had to go somewhere.

**AR:** He's potentially saveable and it takes somebody like Steve Rogers to recognize that.

04

**04** Co-director Joe Russo sets up a shot.

**05** Black Widow makes a perfect foil for Captain America, according to the Russo brothers.

**06** Sebastian Stan goes before the camera as the Winter Solider.

07

08

09

10

## EASTER EGGS

### WINTER SOLDIER CREATOR

One of the scientists helping to reprogram Bucky is actually Ed Brubaker, the man who co-created The Winter Soldier! Not only did he revive the character in the comics, he was the scientist who brought Bucky back in the film, too! His multi-year run on *Captain America* was a huge influence on both the tone and text of the film.

### HONORABLE MENTIONS

While Captain America and the Falcon are interrogating Jasper Sitwell, he mentions one of the men Hydra has been keeping an eye on – Stephen Strange…

### GLOBE-TROTTING

Steve Rogers keeps a journal of things he needs to do and see to catch up with society. Each country the film was released in has a slightly different list.

### CRISS-CROSSED

A mercenary of HYDRA, Brock Rumlow (Crossbones) makes his first appearance in *The Winter Soldier*. By the end, not only is he charred to a crisp, but his criss-crossed gun straps subtley reflect his comics costume.

### …WHEN I LAY MY VENGEANCE UPON THEE

Nick Fury's tombstone reads, "The Path of the Righteous Man, Ezekiel 25:17." This is a reference to the same speech Samuel L. Jackson's character made in one of *Pulp Fiction*'s most famous scenes, and arguably the role that made him the pop culture icon he is today.

### ARROW TO THE NECK

Although Hawkeye isn't actually in the film, you'll notice that Black Widow wears a tiny arrow necklace all throughout the film, symbolizing her link to Clint "Hawkeye" Barton without pushing it into the spotlight.

### SEA LORE

The S.H.I.E.L.D. ship that features in the opening sequence is called the *Lemurian Star*. In Marvel comic book continuity, Lemuria was a continent in the Pacific, which was taken over by the Deviants, a race of monsters created by the Celestials. When the two races came to blows, "The Great Cataclysm" killed off most of the Deviants.

11

12

## END CREDITS SCENES

"This is the age of miracles, Doctor," proclaims Baron Wolfgang von Strucker, as he looks upon twins Wanda and Pietro Maximoff
— Scarlet Witch and Quicksilver. A second scene confirms that Bucky is still alive. He visits an exhibit dedicated to Captain
America and his team of Howling Commandos.

**Significance** The first scene sets up *Avengers: Age of Ultron*, where the twins become unwilling adversaries against Earth's
mightiest heroes. The second scene indicates that Bucky may be able to overcome the mind control he's endured for decades.

**07** Behind the scenes as
Frank Grillo performs a
scene as Brock Rumlow.

**08** Cap's escape route is
blocked by a S.H.I.E.L.D. jet.

**09** Black Widow on the run
from the Winter Soldier.

**10** Steve Rogers faces
tough decisions as his
loyalty to his country
is called into question.

**11** The Winter Soldier takes
Captain America's shield.

**12** A behind-the-scenes
shot captures Captain
America in typically
acrobatic combat.

# GUARDIANS OF THE GALAXY (2014)

## DIRECTED BY: JAMES GUNN

STARRING: Chris Pratt (Peter Quill/Star-Lord), Zoe Saldana (Gamora), Dave Bautista (Drax), Bradley Cooper (Rocket), Vin Diesel (Groot), Karen Gillan (Nebula), Lee Pace (Ronan), Michael Rooker (Yondu Udonta), Djimon Hounsou (Korath), Glenn Close (Nova Prime), John C. Reilly (Rhomann Dey), Benicio Del Toro (Taneleer Tivan), Sean Gunn (Kraglin), Peter Serafinowicz (Garthan Saal)

After the death of his mother, young Peter Quill is abducted by aliens and taken into space. Years later, the adult Quill has joined the Ravagers, an organization of intergalactic pirates with their own code of honor. Angry over his treatment by the Ravagers, Quill embarks on a mission to the planet Morag to recover an artifact known as the Orb, which he plans to sell. He crosses paths with Korath, a Kree warrior who serves Ronan, who also seeks the Orb.

Ronan follows the ancient ways of his warlike race, and believes those who don't should be punished in the harshest manner. With the Kree Empire and Xandar having achieved a fragile peace, Ronan believes his only recourse is to obliterate the Xandarians from existence. To that end, Ronan forges an alliance with Thanos. In exchange for Ronan bringing the Orb to the Mad Titan, Thanos has agreed to destroy the planet Xandar.

Quill obtains the Orb, and attempts to sell it on Xandar. Unable to complete the sale, Quill is attacked by Gamora, who is also working for Ronan. They are captured by the Nova Corps, along with Rocket and Groot. Interned on the prison known as the Kyln, the four team up with another inmate, Drax, and escape.

Gamora reveals she has found a buyer for the Orb, and she agrees to sell it and split the profits among her comrades. Pursued by Ronan's minions, including Gamora's sister Nebula, Quill and company are attacked, and the Orb is stolen.

Ronan double-crosses Thanos and keeps the Orb – which is revealed to contain a powerful Infinity Stone. He uses it to attack Xandar and destroy it. Quill and his fellow Guardians of the Galaxy unite to defeat Ronan using the Power Stone. The Guardians then return the stone to the Xandarians for safekeeping.

## FIRST APPEARANCES OF:

Peter Quill, Gamora, Rocket, Groot, Yondu, Drax, Nebula, Ronan

**01** Korath, servant of Ronan. **02** The Guardians team up for the first time. **03** Gamora's sister, Nebula.

INTERVIEW

## JAMES GUNN

# Chasing the Orb

The writer and director James Gunn helmed the first two *Guardians of the Galaxy* films.

How would you describe *Guardians of the Galaxy*? At its center, it's an action-adventure film, but within that there's a lot of comedy and a lot of drama. I think it's going to be a big surprise for people.

**What was it like putting this huge, A-list cast together?**
It was incredibly exciting. Chris Pratt was exciting because I never thought we'd find the right guy. We screen-tested a lot of people and I knew within a minute of his test that Chris was Star-Lord. Michael Rooker is my good friend and has been in all my movies, and he was so exciting as Yondu. Benicio Del Toro, Glenn Close, and John C. Reilly are some of my favorite actors in the world, and we were fortunate enough to get them to agree to do this insane film.

**What did Zoe Saldana bring to the role of Gamora?**
Zoe influenced her role in more ways than any other cast member. Zoe signed up to the film very early on and she went through a couple of early script drafts with me, in terms of trying to create a character who was both a strong female character but was also very flawed.

**Could you explain to us how you used the soundtrack when you were filming?**
The score is very important. We wrote part of the score ahead of time so we could play the music on the set, allowing the actors to really understand where we were going with it. It also makes shooting a lot more fun.

**It seems like creating this film was a fantastic team effort. Tell us more.**
Exchanging goodbyes at the end of filming got a little teary. Chris Pratt gave me a dinosaur jaw. I got a wrestling belt from Dave Bautista. I got some cigars and a book of horror from Zoe. I got the cast lunchboxes with pictures of themselves on and little quotes from the movie. A lot of people put their heart and soul into making this movie.

**04** James Gunn (middle) about to film a scene with a certain raccoon...

## EASTER EGGS

### MIDDLE OF KNOWHERE
Knowhere is described as being "the head of a celestial being," but Marvel fans know that it's not just any celestial being – it's one of the Celestials. These giants like to turn up at planets harboring sentient life and attempt to spur on their evolution, destroying the life (and planet) if it doesn't meet their standards.

### THE SEARCH IS OVER
While the Collector tells us the history of the Infinity Stones, we also get to witness Eson the Searcher, a Celestial, wielding the Power Stone.

### COSMO-NAUT CANINE
The Head of Security at Knowhere is none other than Cosmo, the famous telepathic dog in a spacesuit! In the comics, although his origin has never been fully explained, he appears to be a Russian cosmonaut who has somehow gained the power of telepathy and set out to make his way in the universe. Here we see him at odds with fellow fleabag Rocket. The two notoriously do not get along…

### COLLECTOR'S NERDVANA
The Collector's menagerie contains an abundance of things from the Marvel Cinematic Universe – a Dark Elf from *Thor: The Dark World*, a Chitauri as seen in *The Avengers*, and we also get a glimpse of the cocoon of Adam Warlock, aka Him, the some-time adversary of Thanos and frequent guardian of the Infinity Gems!

### MALIGNED MALLARD
The infamous Howard the Duck made his Marvel comeback in the final credits scene. The snarky duck previously starred in his own film in 1986.

## END CREDITS SCENES

A tonal shift for the MCU, *Guardians of the Galaxy* blasts off into the cosmos with a mid-credits scene that reflects the movie's fun, comedic, and pop culture influences. Following the defeat of Ronan the Accuser and Groot's sad demise to protect his friends, we see Drax sharpening his knives, with a baby Groot in the foreground being regrown from a tiny remnant of his predecessor. As The Jackson 5's "I Want You Back" plays, Baby Groot throws some shapes, freezing when Drax snaps his head around. As Drax returns to work, Groot can't resist bopping away!

**Significance:** Groot lives! And set to slowly mature…

The final scene takes us back to earlier in the movie, and the detonation of the purple Infinity Stone devastates the Collector's museum. Tivan lies crumpled on the floor when Cosmo the Spacedog licks his face. "What do you let him lick you like that for?" says a gruff voice offscreen, belonging to none other than Howard the Duck!

**Significance:** Howard is voiced by actor Seth Green and reappears in the *Guardians of the Galaxy* sequel partying on Contraxia.

06 Star-Lord, Gamora, and Drax kitted out for a fight.

07 An epic battle lies ahead for the *Milano*, Star-Lord's ship.

08 The alien of few words, i.e., "I am Groot!"

09 Ronan the Accuser: a radical member of the Kree race.

10 Star-Lord's escape attempt gets a little dicey.

11 The warrior Yondu and his trusty arrow.

# AVENGERS AGE OF ULTRON (2015)

## DIRECTED BY: JOSS WHEDON

STARRING : Robert Downey Jr. (Tony Stark/Iron Man), Chris Evans (Steve Rogers/Captain America), Chris Hemsworth (Thor), Scarlett Johansson (Natasha Romanoff/Black Widow), Mark Ruffalo (Bruce Banner/Hulk), Jeremy Renner (Clint Barton/Hawkeye), Samuel L. Jackson (Nick Fury), Don Cheadle (James "Rhodey" Rhodes/War Machine), Aaron Taylor-Johnson (Pietro Maximoff/Quicksilver), Elizabeth Olsen (Wanda Maximoff/Scarlet Witch), Paul Bettany (J.A.R.V.I.S./Vision), Anthony Mackie (Sam Wilson/Falcon), James Spader (Ultron), Andy Serkis (Ulysses Klaue), Thomas Kretschmann (Wolfgang von Strucker), Stellan Skarsgård (Erik Selvig), Claudia Kim (Dr Helen Cho), Idris Elba (Heimdall), Cobie Smulders (Maria Hill)

Following the dissolution of S.H.I.E.L.D. at the end of *Captain America: The Winter Soldier,* the Avengers are now operating on their own authority. They confront a Hydra cell under the command of Wolfgang von Strucker in Sokovia. Strucker has been attempting to harness the power of the same scepter Loki used during the Battle of New York. The Avengers stop Strucker and recover the scepter, but encounter two dangerous new super beings. Called "the twins" by von Strucker, these powerful combatants present a new problem for Earth's mightiest heroes.

Stark and Banner use the scepter to finalize the peacekeeping program codenamed Ultron. The program would put Stark's Iron Legion under the control of an artificial intelligence that could potentially safeguard the world. Ultron comes online, and immediately becomes self-aware. The AI determines that the only way to save the planet is to destroy humanity.

The Avengers defeat the Iron Legion under Ultron's control, save one armor that flees with the scepter. With the help of Pietro and Wanda Maximoff, Ultron creates a drone army to complete his goals. Acquiring vibranium from the mercenary Ulysses Klaue, Ultron also tries to build a perfect android body to house his AI The attempt fails, and out of that experiment, Vision is born.

Ultron plans to effect Earth's demise from Sokovia, by using a device of his own creation to lift the Sokovian capital city into the sky, then drop it, causing an extinction-level event. The Avengers battle relentlessly against wave after wave of Ultron's drones, before they finally manage to stop him. At the end of the fight, Hulk commandeers an Avengers Quinjet, and takes off into space.

## FIRST APPEARANCES OF:

Vision, Ultron, Ulysses Klaue, F.R.I.D.A.Y.

**01** Strucker taking charge of Hydra operations. **02** Cap and Thor working together. **03** Ultron's own legion attack

## SCARLETT JOHANSSON

# Spy-der Woman

Scarlett Johansson reflects on her time with Marvel Studios and the changes that have happened – to her character and to the movies.

**W**hat are your favorite aspects of working on the Marvel Studios films?

It's been really exciting to get to work with some of the actors from different franchises that I have admired, and I guess you could say we are sort of an extended family. And there are new characters that are also being introduced to the family, and that part of it is wonderful.

Certainly, Marvel has really championed hiring actors that are unexpected, dedicated, and fresh. They advocate for new talent, and that part of it is so exciting. I'm proud of what we've built and I'm proud of my character.

**How is it to see more female faces in the group?**

I've been advocating for some more female energy just in the cast and crew as a whole for the better part of a decade. It's been really great to see a more diverse group and certainly great to see that the audiences are begging for and embracing really strong female Super Heroes – or Super Heroines, I should say.

The fans are hungry for these stories, and they also want to see a more diverse group that better represents the population. It's wonderful to feel like you've witnessed and been a part of that growth.

**What have these 10 years meant to you?**

It's been an incredible opportunity for me to be able to continue to come back to a character that I love so much, and be able to peel back the layers of a character that I think reflects myself and reflects my own growth and my own challenges. I really feel it's been a gift as an actor to be able to have that experience. I don't think there are many other opportunities that you have like that in film, to be able to continuously come back to a character that's as complex as Natasha.

I really feel that I've had an incredible opportunity to play this iconic character that means so much to people, and I really have to thank the audiences for that because they embraced my portrayal of her from the beginning. They allowed me to walk in Natasha's shoes and kick ass in them too! It's been great.

**04** Black Widow on an action-packed rescue mission in *Avengers: Age of Ultron*. **05** Scarlett Johansson as Black Widow – one of the deadliest Avengers.

06

# EASTER EGGS

### ARTIFICIAL EASTER EGGS

When Tony Stark is trying to find an AI to replace J.A.R.V.I.S., he tosses aside one labeled "Jocasta." In the comics, Jocasta (first seen in 1977's *Avengers* #162) was the name of Ultron's own creation – a wife whose personality was patterned after the brainwaves of Janet van Dyne. In the comic book universe, Hank Pym, the original Ant-Man, Janet's husband, created Ultron.

### FRIDAY'S CHILD

Stark chooses to replace J.A.R.V.I.S. with the AI called F.R.I.D.A.Y. – possibly a nod to classic film *His Girl Friday*. In the comics, Friday was a holographic assistant who debuted in *Iron Man* Vol. 3 #53 (2002), later developing a crush on Tony before becoming his personal secretary.

### FINELY CRAFTED

According to the visual effects team, Ultron's main appearance is based on a swiss watch, as they wanted him to appear as "The perfect robot: elegant, beautiful, and sophisticated."

### BOW AND ARROW

Hawkeye's newest child, born during the events of *Age of Ultron*, is briefly spotted near the end of the film, and his shirt reveals an Easter Egg of a name – Nathaniel Pietro Barton, named in honor of the man who saved Clint Barton's life, Pietro Maximoff.

### ALL'S FAIR IN LOVE

The Hulkbuster armor is codenamed "Veronica," which is an in-joke based on the popular U.S. *Archie* comics. The lead character, Archie, is torn between two very different women: Betty and Veronica. The Hulk has already got a "Betty" (played by Liv Tyler in *The Incredible Hulk*), so Stark and Banner built the Hulk another "girlfriend": Veronica, the Hulkbuster armor.

### ECHOES OF DISTANT MEMORIES

Stan Lee's cameos are hard to miss, but this movie has another classic Marvel creator in the frame (sort of)... When Captain America has his vision of the past, the band is known as the Roy Thomas Players. Roy Thomas created Ultron and Vision, who made their MCU debuts in this movie.

### EXPECTING THE UNEXPECTED

Scarlett Johansson was pregnant during filming, so many of her scenes were shot early to get as much footage of her as possible. In addition to a lot of CGI being used to cover Johansson's pregnancy up, three stunt doubles were used. Apparently, it was difficult to tell them apart, to the extent where Chris Evans would chat with one of them only to realize halfway through that he wasn't talking to Johansson...

### LITTLE RED ULTRON HOOD

When the twins meet Ultron in Sokovia, he's draped in a red cowl. This is undoubtedly a nod to the way Ultron made his comics debut: he was disguised in a red hood and robes and called himself the Crimson Cowl.

### THE CREATOR

Helen Cho – the scientist responsible for the invention of the regeneration cradle that ultimately allows Vision to be created – is a character from the comics. She's the mother of the popular character, Amadeus Cho. He temporarily took the lead role in the comic book, *Totally Awesome Hulk*.

### WE'RE NOT WORTHY

During the friendly competition to see if any other Avenger is worthy enough to lift Thor's hammer, Black Widow declines to attempt the challenge. In the comic *What If? Age of Ultron* #3, Black Widow successfully lifts the hammer and becomes the Goddess of Thunder.

**06** Elizabeth Olsen as the Scarlet Witch.

**07** Ultron at full power.

**08** The Avengers proving they are Earth's mightiest heroes.

**09** Thanos – ready to take on the Avengers.

## END CREDITS SCENE

In a solitary mid-credits scene, Thanos has grown tired of the successive failures of his minions and decides to take matters into his own hands. Or "hand" in this case, as he reaches into his vault to put on the Infinity Gauntlet: "Fine, I'll do it myself," he affirms.

**Significance:** As Hela later identifies in *Thor: Ragnarok*, the Infinity Gauntlet in Odin's vault in *Thor: The Dark World* was a mere forgery. Having armed himself with the genuine gauntlet, Thanos sets out to fill the six empty slots on it with the universe's Infinity Stones. This is the last we see of Thanos until he reappears in *Avengers: Infinity War* where many Super Heroes and many humans face a devastating fate...

# ANT-MAN (2015)

## DIRECTED BY: PEYTON REED

STARRING: Paul Rudd (Scott Lang/Ant-Man), Michael Douglas (Hank Pym), Evangeline Lilly (Hope Van Dyne), Abby Ryder Fortson (Cassie Lang), Judy Greer (Maggie Lang), Bobby Cannavale (Jim Paxton), Corey Stoll (Darren Cross/Yellowjacket), Anthony Mackie (Sam Wilson/Falcon), Michael Peña (Luis), David Dastmalchian (Kurt), Tip "T.I." Harris (Dave), John Slattery (Howard Stark), Hayley Atwell (Peggy Carter), Martin Donovan (Mitchell Carson)

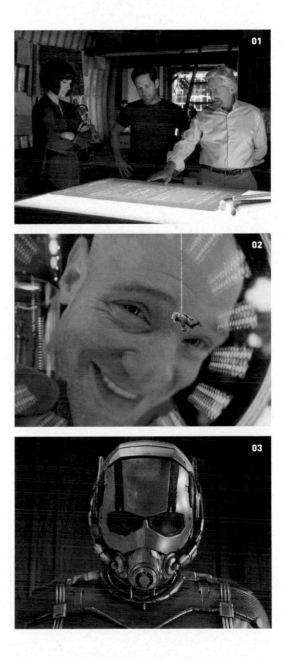

Newly released from prison, Scott Lang visits his daughter Cassie, and promises he won't turn back to crime. After losing his job at Baskin-Robbins, Lang reluctantly accepts a criminal opportunity. Along with his friend Luis, and his roommates Kurt and Dave, Lang raids the home of a wealthy inventor. In the process, Lang displays his wide-ranging knowledge of electronics – as well as his ability to think quickly on his feet – by deactivating the home's impressive, intricate security systems. Finding nothing of value inside the safe, Lang takes the only thing he finds – something that looks like a weird motorcycle suit.

Lang soon discovers that it's not a motorcycle suit, but a shrinking suit that belonged to Dr Hank Pym, the original Ant-Man. Pym recruits Lang to join him and his daughter, Hope Van Dyne, in an effort to prevent Pym's protégé, Darren Cross, from selling the shrinking technology to the highest bidder. Lang trains alongside Van Dyne, who blames her father for her mother's disappearance. Pym reveals that Van Dyne's mother was his partner, the Wasp, and that she gave her life to save her country.

With the help of Luis, Kurt, and Dave, Team Pym prevents Cross from selling the shrinking technology to former Hydra agents. Cross escapes with the shrinking tech, and Lang, as Ant-Man, gives pursuit. Their fight rages over the skies of San Francisco, and they ultimately do battle in miniaturized form on a train table in Lang's daughter's room.

In order to disable Cross' Yellowjacket suit, Lang goes subatomic, shrinking between atoms and wrecking the internal works. The suit shrinks out of control, and Cross literally vanishes from sight. Reunited with his daughter, Lang embarks on a new career as Ant-Man.

## FIRST APPEARANCES OF:

Scott Lang, Hank Pym, Hope Van Dyne, Janet Van Dyne, Cassie Lang, Darren Cross/Yellowjacket, Luis, Kurt, Dave

**01** Scott, Hank, and Hope make an unstoppable team. **02** Darren Cross teases Ant-Man with the Yellowjacket suit. **03** Ant-Man suited up.

INTERVIEW

## PAUL RUDD

# There Are No Small Parts

Stepping into the character of Ant-Man, Paul Rudd brought plenty of his lovable charisma that everyone knows and adores. But his role in the making of the film went even deeper than just being the leading man...

So not only did you star in the film, but you were also one of the writers. Tell us about that process.
Well, the one thing that it does when you work on the script of the movie is it just gives you much more of an insight into all of the characters. You're thinking about their motivations, you're thinking about their storylines, how every decision *your* character makes affects theirs. So I had a much more comprehensive understanding of the story than I did when I first signed on when I wasn't a writer on the film.

When you weren't writing, you were fighting, like the scene where Evangeline Lilly teaches your character how to punch.
We knew that Scott Lang was gonna have to go through a training sequence to learn how to really become Ant-Man. But one of the things that I do kind of like is that I just get my butt kicked by Evangeline over and over again, and that she's like, the best, the toughest one in the movie. So you know, Scott learns how to fight, like really fight, from her. She's just tough!

Tell us a little about the Ant-Man suit.
The suit is deceptive in its complexity! Not just the parts, but how certain things work. There are hundreds of pieces [to the suit] and it takes a while to get into it – I need a small pit crew to help me. It takes about half an hour, I'd say. It doesn't breathe that much. It doesn't have any of those cold packs built into it. But who needs that when you're filming in Georgia in the summer? Thankfully we've been shooting on these soundstages for a lot of it, and early on they kept these things like a meat locker. It was really cold and it helped!

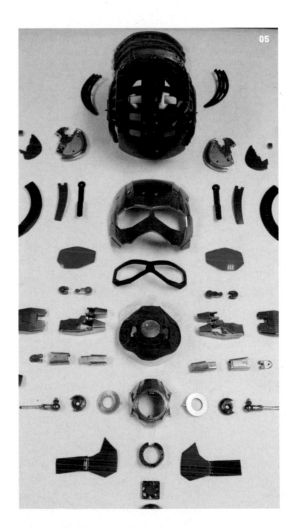

**04** Paul Rudd as master cat-burglar, Scott Lang. **05** Warning: All of the small intricate pieces of Ant-Man's suit may be a choking hazard.

**06** Scott Lang: an ant's best friend.

**07** Peggy Carter helped Hank Pym develop the Ant-Man suit.

**08** Darren Cross, Pym's protégé-turned-villain.

**09** Yellowjacket strikes!

**10** Hank reveals a secret to his daughter...

**11** ...A new Wasp suit!

09

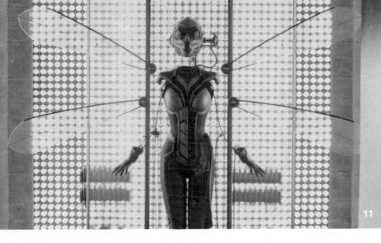

10

11

## EASTER EGGS

### MEETING MR MILGROM
After being fired, Lang returns to his hotel "The Milgrom Hotel," presumably named for multitalented Marvel staffer Al Milgrom. Milgrom had no direct connection with Ant-Man, but he did draw *West Coast Avengers* (in which Hank Pym appeared) and he inked all of *A-Next*, which featured the first appearance of Hope Van Dyne.

### OLD MEETS NEW
During Scott Lang's first outing as Ant-Man, he crashes onto the top of a parked car. The driver of this car is Garrett Morris, a comedian who played Ant-Man in a classic *Saturday Night Live* sketch – the first live-action appearance of the Super Hero.

### IT TRULY IS A SMALL WORLD
While posing as a guard, Michael Peña whistles the classic song "It's A Small World (After All)" from the eponymous Disney ride, an obvious nod to Ant-Man's powers.

### AN ASTONISHING REFERENCE
Darren Cross refers to shrinking technology as "Propaganda. Tales to astonish." *Tales to Astonish* was the title of the 1960s series where Hank Pym (then Ant-Man) and Janet Van Dyne (the Wasp) first appeared.

### ECHOES FROM THE PAST
During the scene where Scott Lang shrinks down into the Quantum Realm, a silhouette appears before him very briefly. The figure has four wings, suggesting it's Janet Van Dyne, the original Wasp, stuck in this microverse.

### PEW-PEW
Yellowjacket's suit fires lasers that use the same sound effect as the AT-AT's main gun in the *Star Wars* movies.

### GOOD OR EVIL?
Although Hope Van Dyne is a hero in the Marvel Cinematic Universe, in the comics she is the villain known as Red Queen. After her parents' deaths, Hope and her twin brother Henry Pym Jr. use the money left to them to create the Super Villain team the Revengers.

### NO ARTIFICIAL COLOURS
Posters for the Brazilian green soda "Pingo Doce" can be seen at certain points in the film throughout San Francisco. Bruce Banner worked for the Pingo Doce company in *The Incredible Hulk*.

### THE ON-SET PICNIC
During the filming, it was Michael Douglas' 70th birthday. The cast and crew celebrated on set by bringing him a birthday cake in the form of a film reel with ants crawling over it.

## END CREDITS SCENES

Having been forced to watch Lang play hero in the Ant-Man suit throughout the film, in the mid-credits scene, Hope is given her own advanced Wasp prototype suit by her father that he'd begun working on with his wife. "It's about damn time," she says.

**Significance:** The scene heralds the birth of a new Wasp – but on a meta level, Hope's "about damn time" could refer to the fact that this movie's sequel, *Ant-Man and the Wasp*, is the first Marvel Studios movie to include a female character in the title.

The post-credits scene is a clip taken from the forthcoming *Captain America: Civil War*. Falcon and Captain America have Bucky in their custody. Unable to depend on Stark (for reasons that become apparent), Falcon suggests a guy he knows, referring to the tiny hero he encounters when Lang tries to steal a device from Avengers headquarters earlier in *Ant-Man*.

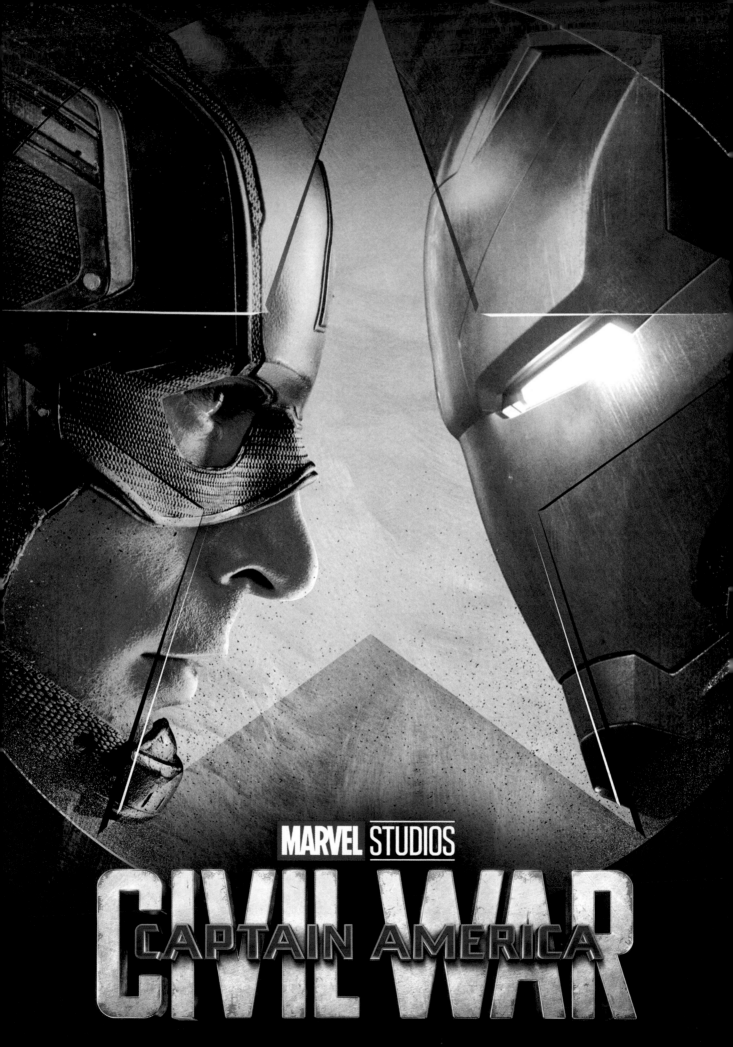

# CAPTAIN AMERICA: CIVIL WAR (2016)

## DIRECTED BY: ANTHONY RUSSO, JOE RUSSO

STARRING: Chris Evans (Steve Rogers/Captain America), Robert Downey Jr. (Tony Stark/Iron Man), Sebastian Stan (James Buchanan "Bucky" Barnes/Winter Soldier), Scarlett Johansson (Natasha Romanoff/ Black Widow), Don Cheadle (James "Rhodey" Rhodes/War Machine), Anthony Mackie (Sam Wilson/ Falcon), Jeremy Renner (Clint Barton/Hawkeye), Chadwick Boseman (T'Challa/Black Panther), Paul Bettany (Vision), Elizabeth Olsen (Wanda Maximoff/Scarlet Witch), Paul Rudd (Scott Lang/Ant-Man), Tom Holland (Peter Parker/Spider-Man), Emily Vancamp (Sharon Carter), Martin Freeman (Everett K. Ross), William Hurt (Secretary of State Thaddeus Ross), Marisa Tomei (May Parker), John Kani (King T'Chaka), John Slattery (Howard Stark), Hope Davis (Maria Stark), Daniel Brühl (Helmut Zemo), Frank Grillo (Brock Rumlow/Crossbones)

In Lagos, Nigeria, Captain America leads the new incarnation of the Avengers against Brock Rumlow, a former S.H.I.E.L.D./Hydra agent. Rumlow stole a chemical weapon before being apprehended by the Avengers. In the process, Wanda Maximoff briefly loses control of her abilities, resulting in the deaths of several relief workers from Wakanda.

In the wake of that disaster, Secretary of State Thaddeus Ross informs the Avengers that they must sign the Sokovia Accords, which will place the Avengers under the control of an international panel. Tony Stark feels it's the only way for the team to move forward, while Steve Rogers fears this may lead to the Avengers being used for nefarious purposes.

The Accords are to be signed in Vienna, Austria, when a terrorist bomb – believed to have been set off by the Winter Soldier – explodes, taking the life of King T'Chaka of Wakanda. Rogers takes off in search of Bucky Barnes, and T'Chaka's son, T'Challa, joins the hunt.

Stark wants Barnes turned over to the authorities, while Rogers intends to take him to Siberia in pursuit of Helmut Zemo, who he believes was behind the bomb in Vienna. An epic clash between two teams of heroes (Captain America, Hawkeye, Falcon, Scarlet Witch, Ant-Man, and the Winter Soldier on one side; Iron Man, Vision, Spider-Man, Black Widow, Black Panther, and War Machine on the other) takes place in Berlin, and Rogers escapes with Barnes.

In Siberia, Rogers and Barnes are joined by Stark, who has learned that Barnes was not responsible for the bombing. Zemo reveals that Barnes was, however, responsible for the deaths of Stark's parents, sending Stark into a rage. Rogers and Stark fight, with Rogers barely winning.

## FIRST APPEARANCES OF:

T'Challa/Black Panther, King T'Chaka, Spider-Man, Everett K. Ross, Baron Zemo

01 The search for Hydra agent Crossbones leads to an explosive incident that could spell the end for the Avengers.
02 Black Panther, Vision, Iron Man, Black Widow, and War Machine attempt to persuade their fellow heroes to register themselves. 03 Hawkeye, Scarlet Witch, and Captain America resist arrest.

## SEBASTIAN STAN

# A Winter Soldier's Tale

The assassin known as the Winter Soldier is played by actor Sebastian Stan.
Here he reflects on his journey back from the Hydra brainwash...

What does Bucky think about Steve after their battle in *Captain America: The Winter Soldier*?

At this point, Bucky is learning about his past in the way a student learns a subject. He doesn't have it figured out at the start, but it builds throughout the movie. He begins to realize that, to some extent, Steve Rogers is his only hope and the only other person who is also from another time and place. Cap is the only friend he's got.

How does Bucky cope with his past?

Both Cap and Bucky are dealing with serious post-traumatic issues and incredible guilt. Steve is haunted by the fact he didn't go after Bucky when he fell from the train; he's suffering from survivor's guilt. Bucky's guilt is on another level because he's learning about the killing machine he has become, and how much damage he has done over the years.

Did you enjoy filming the action scenes in *Captain America: Civil War*?

It was challenging, but it gets easier with experience. Although sometimes you need to put your ego aside and let the stunt team do their job, because these guys do it best. I'm happy though, because I feel like they allowed me to do a lot of stunts, which is fantastic.

What was your favorite moment of *Captain America: Civil War*?

I really enjoyed filming the flashback sequences. We got to see in more depth what happened to the Winter Soldier and what the world was like for him. I also liked the ambiguous scenes where I got to go back and forth between Bucky and the Winter Soldier. Ultimately in *Civil War*, you got a very real sense of just how dangerous the Winter Soldier is.

**04** The Winter Soldier feels the claws of the Black Panther as Scarlet Witch comes to his aid.
**05** Bucky Barnes: triggered into becoming an assassin.

## EASTER EGGS

### NEVER BACK DOWN

Captain America tells Iron Man, "I could do this all day," which is a direct callback to *Captain America: The First Avenger*, when pre-Super-Soldier Serum Steve Rogers tells his attackers (and later, as Cap, the Red Skull) exactly the same thing.

### SPEECH

The speech given by Sharon Carter at her aunt Peggy's funeral about standing your ground is partly taken from a speech Cap himself gives to Peter Parker in *The Amazing Spider-Man* #537, part of the *Civil War* comics storyline.

### THE MARVEL COMMUNITY

Jim Rash from *Community* makes an appearance as someone similar to his character, Dean Pelton. He's the eager MIT staff member who asks if the new grant is available to staff research projects as well.

### OUT OF THE DIRECTOR'S CHAIR

Dr. Broussard, the psychiatrist killed and replaced by Zemo so that he can get to Bucky, is played by Joe Russo, one of the film's directing duo.

### YOU CAN'T HANDLE THE BLUTH

If you're a fan of *Arrested Development*, you can spot a Bluth Stair Car in the background during the airport fight scene.

### DISNEY PRISON

The strange cube-like prison that holds Bucky is labeled D23, sharing the name of Disney's fan-club, which stands for "Disney 1923" – the year the studio was founded.

### STRIKING A POSE

The film includes visual references to the *Civil War* comics event, such as Steve McNiven's Cap vs. Iron Man cover image, and a shot of the opposing teams facing each other.

### FLYING ANT

Ant-Man sitting on an arrow fired by Hawkeye is a reference to a famous *Avengers* cover – *Avengers* #223, by Ed Hannigan and Klaus Janson.

### RAGING ANT

When Ant-Man is psyching himself up to turn into Giant-Man, he repeats over and over to himself, "I'm the boss, I'm the boss…" a reference to Robert De Niro in the final scene of *Raging Bull*.

**06** Captain America leads the charge as the heroes clash.

**07** Vision comes to the aid of Scarlet Witch.

**08** Spider-Man gets to grips with War Machine as the battle heats up.

**09** Steve tries to stop Bucky escaping by helicopter.

**10** Captain America and Iron Man engage in a climactic battle.

## END CREDITS SCENES

In the mid-credits scene, we see Bucky Barnes taken to the African nation, Wakanda. "You know, if they find out he's here, they'll come for him," says Steve Rogers. "Let them try," replies the king, T'Challa.

In the post-credits scene, Peter Parker returns home to Queens, New York with a bruised eye. He tells his Aunt May that he was punched by a guy named Steve from Brooklyn. Peter shines a red light from his web-shooter on the ceiling, revealing a spider-signal projection.

**Significance:** The first scene introduces audiences to Wakanda for the first time. The second leads directly into *Spider-Man: Homecoming*.

08

09

10

# *DOCTOR STRANGE* (2016)

## DIRECTED BY: **SCOTT DERRICKSON**

STARRING: Benedict Cumberbatch (Doctor Stephen Strange), Rachel McAdams (Doctor Christine Palmer), Tilda Swinton (the Ancient One), Chiwetel Ejiofor (Mordo), Benedict Wong (Wong), Mads Mikkelsen (Kaecilius), Michael Stuhlbarg (Doctor Nicodemus West), Benjamin Bratt (Jonathan Pangborn), Chris Hemsworth (Thor)

Doctor Stephen Strange, an arrogant surgeon, is involved in a terrible car accident. When he awakens, he finds out that his hands were badly injured in the crash and will never fully heal. Strange refuses to accept that he will never be able to operate again. Searching desperately for a cure, he learns of a formerly paralyzed man, Jonathan Pangborn, who traveled to a place called Kamar-Taj and recovered his ability to walk.

Strange makes the trek to Kamar-Taj in Nepal, where he meets Mordo, who introduces him to the Ancient One. The Ancient One reveals the world of magic to Strange, opening his eyes to concepts of astral projection and multiple dimensions. The Ancient One agrees to teach Strange the ways of the mystic arts, and he proves to be an apt pupil.

While Strange moves up through the ranks, a threat looms in the form of Kaecilius and his zealots. Kaecilius has stolen a page from the Book of Cagliostro – a dark spell intended to summon the dreaded Dormammu to our world. Once Kaecilius starts the spell, it brings disaster to Kamar-Taj and the other Sanctum Sanctorums in England, New York, and Hong Kong.

The Ancient One does her best to stop Kaecilius in New York. Her efforts fall short, however, as she's cut down by her foe. She perishes, leaving Strange to rally the other Masters of the Mystic Arts.

Strange faces Kaecilius, and ultimately Dormammu, using the Eye of Agamotto to trap Dormammu in a time loop until he agrees to leave Earth alone. With the threat of Dormammu and Kaecilius gone, Strange takes up residence in the New York Sanctum Sanctorum.

## FIRST APPEARANCES OF:

Doctor Stephen Strange, the Ancient One, Wong, Mordo, Kaecilius, Dormammu

**01** Strange reluctantly takes instruction. **02** The Ancient One wields her mystical powers. **03** Doctor Strange meets his opponent in the Dark Dimension.

INTERVIEW

## BENEDICT CUMBERBATCH

# Mastering the Mystic Arts

_Doctor Strange_ introduces audiences to the mind-bending worlds of the Mystic Arts. Benedict Cumberbatch reflects on his time as the master of the Time Stone.

Can you tell us about the journey your character, Doctor Strange, undertakes?

This man has been utterly destroyed by a car accident that has taken away the dexterity of his hands through irreparable damage. A chance conversation leads him to meet someone who journeyed to Kathmandu in search of a cure for their almost-complete paralysis. Incredibly, while they were there, their condition was reversed. This gives Stephen Strange a tiny chink of light and he follows it. However, he is an arrogant, self-serving, materialistic Westerner who has been caught in a soulless reality. At his core, he lacks a spirit and a soul. He embarks on this journey in order to recover the use of his hands but, in fact, what he has to do is become the person he never was. This is the end of Stephen Strange's old life and the beginning of his new life as a Master of the Mystic Arts.

Have you used any of the classic comic book stories to inform your role?

Yes, the comics have been incredibly useful. Obviously you have very different writers and artists who have worked on this character through the decades, but they've remained pretty loyal to the basic ingredients. I've gleaned a lot from that, whether it's his humor, drive, or how he uses his hands to cast spells and hold demons and gods in his power. The comics are also beautifully drawn and visually rich. That immediately translates into the cinematic landscape. There's a lot of real-world live action in this film but there's also the fantastical adventure element. The variety of environments we filmed in and the action that takes place in those environments is exceptional.

What makes this the right time for Doctor Strange to join the Marvel Cinematic Universe?

He is a big presence in the original comics, but he's flown under the radar within the MCU until now. The MCU has an ever-expanding group of Super Heroes that are relatable, if slightly extraordinary. From that, everything blossoms into something more surreal, so you have wormholes opening up over New York and otherworldly destruction happening within the world's space and time. But it's about to explode into other dimensions, and Strange is a very natural bridge between that. I love every single moment of it.

**04** Strange – humbled before the Eye of Agamotto. **05** The Sanctum Sanctorum where Doctor Strange resides and protects the world.

## EASTER EGGS

### YOU'RE THE WONG THAT I WAND

The wand that Wong uses in the final battle (with a horned head at either end) is recognizable as the Wand of Watoomb from the comics. The wand enhances the wielder's magic energies.

### EYE OF AVALON

Another artifact that Doctor Strange wields is the Evil Eye, an offensive/defensive magical tool first seen in *Fantastic Four #54* (1966).

### STRANGER THAN BENEDICT-ION

Believe it or not, Dormammu's motion capture was performed by none other than Benedict Cumberbatch.

### MINDLESS APPEARANCE

When Kaecilius and his followers are sucked into the Dark Dimension, they become dark, almost featureless beings with a single glowing eye, very much resembling the savage and powerful Mindless Ones – mystical beings who first appeared in *Strange Tales #127* (1964).

### TRIBUNAL TRIBUTE

Mordo makes use of the weapon known as the Staff of the Living Tribunal, which refers to one of the most powerful entities in the entire Marvel Comics universe.

### GUARDIAN GHOST

Daniel Drumm, the original Guardian of the New York Sanctum, is better known to comics fans as the sibling of Brother Voodoo. In the comics, Drumm's ghost is mystically bound to his brother.

### NO PATIENTS

Doctor Strange is offered a patient described as a 35--year-old Air Force colonel who crushed his spine in an experimental suit of armor. Director Scott Derrickson has claimed that it's *not* James Rhodes, aka War Machine – and in fairness, the timeline doesn't line up. (Fans have also speculated that it might be the man who was twisted in half by Justin Hammer's experimental armor during *Iron Man 2*.)

### MUSIC MANIA

On the road, Strange plays a Pink Floyd track – "Interstellar Overdrive." Pink Floyd's second album, *A Saucerful Of Secrets*, actually had Doctor Strange on the cover!

### RUNAWAY WIZARD

A character in the Hong Kong Sanctum is credited as Tina Minoru – the mother of Nico Minoru, of the Runaways. The staff she grabs is clearly the Staff of One, which allows its user to cast any spell they can imagine – but only once. Tina is portrayed by Brittany Ishibashi in Hulu's *Runaways* TV show.

06

07

**06** Strange sees into his soul.

**07** The twisting nature of realities.

**08** Doctor Strange primed to face his foe.

**09** Kaecilius is composed and ready to fight.

**10** The Ancient One has a final lesson.

**11** The first look at the mysterious power of the Ancient One.

## END CREDITS SCENES

Doctor Strange welcomes Thor into the New York Sanctum Sanctorum as he searches for Odin. As a Master of the Mystic Arts, Stephen Strange keeps a watchlist of beings from other realms that pose a threat to Earth, with Loki being one such menace.

**Significance:** After spellbinding Thor with a magically refilling tankard of mead, Doctor Strange is eager to remove Loki from New York, and so offers his help to Thor, confirming the sorcerer's place in *Thor: Ragnarok* and providing a hint of the humorous tone to be expected from the God of Thunder's forthcoming adventure.

The second credits scene features disillusioned sorcerer Mordo on a violent quest for justice, having discovered that his mentor, the Ancient One, used magic from the villainous Dormammu. Mordo is in search of sorcerers who he believes are perverting nature, and steals the magic of a former disciple of the Ancient One, Jonathan Pangborn, who used her teachings to cure his paraplegia.

**Significance:** This scene potentially forms a set-up for a future *Doctor Strange* film.

08

09

10

11

MARVEL STUDIOS

GUARDIANS
OF
THE GALAXY
VOL. 2

# GUARDIANS OF THE GALAXY VOL. 2 (2016)

## DIRECTED BY: JAMES GUNN

STARRING: Chris Pratt (Peter Quill/Star-Lord), Zoe Saldana (Gamora), Dave Bautista (Drax),
Bradley Cooper (Rocket), Vin Diesel (Groot), Karen Gillan (Nebula), Michael Rooker (Yondu Udonta),
Sean Gunn (Kraglin), Pom Klementieff (Mantis), Kurt Russell (Ego), Laura Haddock (Meredith Quill),
Chris Sullivan (Taserface), Sylvester Stallone (Stakar Ogord), Michael Rosenbaum (Martinex),
Ving Rhames (Charlie-27), Michelle Yeoh (Aleta Ogord)

The Guardians of the Galaxy agree to destroy a creature known as the Abilisk in order to defend Anulax Batteries that belong to the Sovereign. The Guardians uphold their end of the bargain; in exchange, the Sovereign turn over Nebula, whom they had captured previously. En route from the Sovereign homeworld, Rocket reveals that he has stolen a few Anulax Batteries. The Sovereign follow and attack, forcing the *Milano* to crash on a nearby planet.

While Rocket and Groot remain behind to fix the *Milano*, Peter Quill, Gamora, and Drax meet and follow Ego, an extraterrestrial being who claims to be Quill's father. Along with Ego's companion Mantis, they travel back to Ego's world. Ego reveals that Quill can utilize the power within Ego's world, like his father, and use it to create worlds.

Meanwhile, Yondu Udonta and his Ravagers have been hired by the Sovereign to capture the Guardians. They find Rocket and Groot, and capture them (with the help of Nebula). There's a mutiny among the Ravagers when Yondu won't commit to turning Quill over to the Sovereign.

Nebula travels to Ego's planet to kill her sister, Gamora, but the two reach a truce after a prolonged battle. The rivalry between the two sisters has caused each tremendous pain and anguish, and has been stoked by Thanos. Nebula is driven to seek revenge against their adoptive "father."

Ego reveals that he caused the cancer that took the life of Quill's mother so Quill would leave Earth and come to him. He needs Quill to access the power within his world, activating seedlings Ego has placed on planets around the galaxy (including Earth), that will eventually wipe them out. Quill fights back and, with the help of the Guardians, Yondu, Mantis, and Nebula, Ego is defeated.

## FIRST APPEARANCES OF:

Ego, Mantis, Stakar Ogord, Aleta Ogord,
Martinex, Charlie-27, Taserface

**01** Drax aims to destroy the Abilisk from within. **02** Mantis reveals Quill's emotions with just a touch. **03** Michael Rooker as Yondu

INTERVIEW

## KAREN GILLAN

# A Sibling Scorned

Filled with fury, Nebula resents Thanos's adoration of Gamora and looks for revenge against her adoptive sister. Karen Gillen speaks about her expanded role in the Marvel Cinematic Universe.

**H**ow excited were you to become a part of these films?
First of all, I couldn't believe that Nebula would ever enter into the Avengers environment. I'm actually shocked that Nebula lasted so many *Guardians* movies! So I was over the moon at that. It's just such an exciting storyline that my character gets, and it's all linked into Thanos, her father. And so it feels like these seeds have been planted for literally years now. It's exciting to see them all come together.

**What is going on with these characters?**
Nebula has always had a clear agenda throughout the *Guardians* movies, which is to seek revenge on her father Thanos because of the abuse that she has suffered and the terrible upbringing that he inflicted on her. So to see that intertwine into the whole Avengers storyline is pretty satisfying for me; just because that's something I've always been playing with as an actor.

**Where is her relationship with Gamora at?**
At the end of *Guardians of the Galaxy Vol. 2*, Nebula and Gamora have somewhat of a breakthrough where they kind of start to empathize with each other a little bit and understand where each other is coming from and their points of view. And through that they have a physical embrace, which I think Nebula has never experienced.

When we pick it up in the *Avengers* movies they've definitely made progress, but they're still separated. And so they have to try and express to each other where they end up, which is working together as sisters.

**Is it fun to play Nebula more integrated into the group?**
It's so much fun to see Nebula finally have the sense of family that I think she always craved. Ever since she was a kid she just wanted her sister, but she was forced to fight her. She has her hesitations about entering into any sort of family scenario. So it's good to see her working in a team environment with people that are essentially her new family.

**Is it fun to play such a strong female character?**
I love playing a character that is, first of all, physically really strong. That just feels cool and empowering. And she's emotionally strong in ways, but also very damaged emotionally. So she has strengths and weaknesses like any other person. And that's what's interesting. I don't want to play just a strong female. I think we're at the point now where we need a bit more variety than that. And that is exactly what Marvel movies are supplying us with. So that makes me happy.

**04** Nebula – sworn frenemy of the Guardians of the Galaxy. **05** Nebula's life has always been a solitary one.

## EASTER EGGS

### COCOON COLLECTION
Mentioned in the post-credits scene, a cocoon holding "Adam" was seen in the Collector's museum in the first *Guardians of the Galaxy* film and also in *Thor: The Dark World*.

### DANCE-OFF
One fun appearance in the film is the Grandmaster from *Thor: Ragnarok*, who is seen dancing to the song "Guardians Inferno" as the credits roll.

### PUTTING THE GANG BACK TOGETHER
Starhawk/Stakar Ogord (played by Sylvester Stallone) and his team of Ravagers, were the original team of Guardians in the comics. The movie versions appear to have entirely different backstories.

### I'M NOT CRYING, YOU'RE CRYING!
When Peter Quill looks through the Zune that Yondu left for him, the song that's lined up to play is "Father and Son" by Cat Stevens. This most likely means that this was the last song Yondu listened to before he came to save Peter. Ego may have been Peter's father, but we all know who his real daddy was.

### WITH A COUPLE OF SPACE MODIFICATIONS...
Star-Lord uses a device to detect extra-dimensional beings. The prop is actually a heavily modified 1977 Mattel electronic handheld football game, which was very popular around the Christmas period when it was released. The beeping sounds from the device are actual sounds from the game device.

### OLD TECH
Russell Bobbitt, the Prop Master for the film, had to find a replacement for the Sony Walkman headphones as the ones used in the first movie broke during the gap between shooting the films. He made contact with Sony to see if they had any replacements, but they didn't. His only option left was to make six himself from scratch.

### NOT SO HUMAN AFTER ALL...
Mantis was originally a human being in the comics, and acquired her skills by living with the Kree. James Gunn decided that he preferred Star-Lord being the only human character in the team, so he changed her character to be an alien instead.

### COLOR CODED
At the beginning of the film, Ego is driving a car that is painted metallic blue with orange details. Peter Quill's ship, the *Milano*, has the same color scheme.

06

07

08

## END CREDITS SCENES

The most poignant of the credits scenes features the "original" Guardians of the Galaxy team as they appeared in the comics, led by Stakar Ogord. Yondu's funeral reunites the old team, including Aleta Ogord, Martinex, Charlie-27, Krugarr, and Mainframe.

**Significance:** Could we see the original team return in the future?

In a second scene, Priestess Ayesha plans to set her new creation upon the treacherous Guardians – named "Adam"...

**Significance:** This artificial being is believed to be Adam Warlock, a powerful, gold-skinned 'perfect human' who debuted in the comics in 1967.

The bevy of scenes is rounded off with a Stan Lee cameo where he is seen speaking with the Watchers – a race of extraterrestrial observers of the universe – and alludes to his many appearances across the MCU.

**Significance:** This goes some way to explain Stan Lee's roles in every MCU movie, playing to a fan theory that he is the same character in each film!

**06** The *Quadrant* blasts a hole into the planet surface.

**07** Ayesha sits high and mighty on her throne.

**08** Zoe Saldana undergoes heavy make-up prosthetics.

**09** Close friends: Rocket and Groot.

**10** Ego shows Quill his potential.

**11** Yondu experiences the trouble with space travel.

# *THOR: RAGNAROK* (2017)

## DIRECTED BY: **TAIKA WAITITI**

STARRING: Chris Hemsworth (Thor), Mark Ruffalo (Bruce Banner/Hulk), Benedict Cumberbatch (Doctor Strange), Tom Hiddleston (Loki), Anthony Hopkins (Odin), Idris Elba (Heimdall), Cate Blanchett (Hela), Karl Urban (Skurge), Jeff Goldblum (Grandmaster), Tessa Thompson (Valkyrie), Zachary Levi (Fandral), Tadanobu Asano (Hogun), Ray Stevenson (Volstagg), Taika Waititi (voice of Korg)

Following his vision at the Water of Sights in *Avengers: Age of Ultron*, Thor has been searching through space for the Infinity Stones. Along the way, he has allowed himself to be captured by the Fire Giant Surtur in Muspelheim. Surtur warns Thor that Ragnarok (the end of Asgard) is coming. Thor breaks free, takes Surtur's crown (thus preventing Ragnarok from occurring, or so he believes), and returns to Asgard.

There, he finds Loki has been impersonating Odin. He takes his brother to Earth, and with the help of Doctor Strange, locates Odin in Norway. Near death, Odin reveals that Thor and Loki have a sister, Hela, and upon Odin's death, she will be released from her prison and come to claim Asgard for her own. Odin dies, and Hela appears. The brothers attempt to stop her, but Hela destroys Thor's hammer, Mjolnir. Loki summons the Bifrost to bring them home, and Hela follows, knocking both out of its beam.

On Asgard, Hela kills the Warriors Three, and decimates the Asgardian Army. She assumes power in Asgard, and begins draining the life force of her new subjects for her own needs. Meanwhile, Thor finds himself on a strange world, and falls prisoner to the Grandmaster. He's forced to combat the Grandmaster's "precious champion" in exchange for his freedom. The "precious champion" turns out to be Hulk, who has been living on Sakaar for the last two years.

With the aid of Hulk (then Banner) and Valkyrie, Thor escapes from Sakaar. Using a ship stolen from the Grandmaster, they travel to Asgard to stop Hela. Meanwhile, Heimdall, Loki, and a ship full of refugees from Sakaar buy time for the Asgardians to leave their home. The sudden arrival of Surtur brings more chaos, and the coming of Ragnarok. The Asgardians depart, watching as Surtur and Hela destroy one another, and along with them, Asgard itself.

## FIRST APPEARANCES OF:

Valkyrie, Hela, Korg, Surtur, the Grandmaster, Skurge

**01** Surtur issues a prophetic warning to a captured Thor. **02** Hela leads the attack on Asgard. **03** A freshly shorn Thor perpares for gladiatorial combat.

## MARK RUFFALO

# The Man and the Monster

Mark Ruffalo's sensitive portrayal of Bruce Banner stands in contrast to his performance as Hulk. A co-starring role in *Thor: Ragnarok* gave the actor the chance to exercise his comedic muscles.

Is it difficult playing both Banner and Hulk?
I get to play two totally different characters, which is really fun. Hulk has changed. There's not that component of rage all the time. So he's doing normal things now. He has to eat. He has to bathe. He sleeps – all the things Hulk never did because you don't do that when you're in a full rage, right?

What kind of relationship does Hulk have with Banner in *Thor: Ragnarok*?
It's as contentious as hell. They're in absolute opposition to each other, but we keep hearing Banner repeating a slightly different version of the same lines that Hulk has in his personality. The blur between Hulk and Banner is really wide, but they still meet somewhere. There is a line between them that meets. So there's a lot that they share in common, and I think that's the key to the future of Hulk and Banner's relationship.

Did you enjoy working with Chris Hemsworth?
Chris is as close to a god as you could possibly get, I think. He's talented. He's beautiful. He's supersmart. He's strong. He's a great actor, and he's fun. And he's a physical genius. And what's really fun about *Thor: Ragnarok* is he just broke loose. I think it was great for Chris because he's getting to do things in this movie that he'd never been able to do. And he kind of recreated the character as well.

What did you like about Hulk's relationship with Thor?
Thor just happens to run into Hulk... which is good luck for Thor, because he needs Hulk at this moment to save Asgard. But at a very inopportune moment, Hulk turns back to Banner, and he can't get Hulk back again!

04

**04** Mark Ruffalo as Bruce Banner. **05** The Hulk in gladiator gear.

## EASTER EGGS

### SEEING DOUBLE

Near the start of *Thor: Ragnarok*, a short play is performed in Asgard, starring Matt Damon as Loki, Sam Neill as Odin, and Luke Hemsworth (Chris' brother) as Thor.

### RAGNAROK AND ROLL

Bruce Banner's Duran Duran shirt, originally belonging to Stark, features artwork from the album *Rio* which includes the song "Hungry Like the Wolf" – foreshadowing his battle later with the Fenris Wolf.

### GLADIATORS, ARE YOU READY?

There are multiple Easter Eggs outside of the Sakaarian gladiator arena. The faces of Beta Ray Bill (an alien in the comics who is worthy to wield Thor's hammer), Bi-Beast (a two-headed android that battled Hulk in the comics), and Ares, God of War (who appeared in the *Thor* comics).

### WHEN YOU WISH UPON A RAGNAROK

When Hulk enters the arena, Thor's line "He's a friend from work!" was a suggestion to Chris Hemsworth from a Make-A-Wish child who paid a visit to the set on the day that scene was filmed.

### DIDN'T MAKE THE CUT

In the first trailer for *Thor: Ragnarok*, the scene where Thor meets Hela is shown to be in New York, where the scene was originally meant to be set. Taika Waititi changed it to be set in Norway, which seemed like a more appropriate place for a gathering of the Norse Gods.

### THROG THE FROG

Loki's play references an incident where Loki turned Thor into a frog. This is a callback to a story in the comics where Loki briefly turned Thor into a frog, becoming Throg the Frog of Thunder.

### SCRAPPER 142

Valkyrie is referred to as "Scrapper 142." One of the most famous versions of the Valkyrie character first appeared in *The Incredible Hulk* #142.

### STARCROSSED BROTHERS

At San Diego Comic-Con it was revealed that the Grandmaster and the Collector are, in fact, brothers.

### NO HARD FEELINGS, POINT BREAK

After the computer on the S.H.I.E.L.D. ship fails to recognize Thor as "The Strongest Avenger," he instead tries "Point Break," which Tony Stark called him in the original *Avengers* film due to his resemblance to Patrick Swayze in said film. It works, and the ship comes to life.

**06** Thor and Hulk enjoy a work reunion!

**07** Korg (voiced by Taika Waititi) makes a break for freedom.

**08** Loki fights Valkyrie.

**09** The return of Hela spells the end for Asgard.

**10** Director Taika Waititi works with Jeff Goldblum, a.k.a The Grandmaster.

## END CREDITS SCENES

In the mid-credits scene, Thor commandeers the Grandmaster's ship, the *Statesman*, and heads for Earth with the remainder of his people, the Revengers, the Sakaar refugees, and Loki. While Loki feels it's unwise to take him to a planet where he is reviled, Thor is more optimistic. "I wouldn't worry, brother. I feel like everything's going to work out fine," he says, as Thanos' massive *Sanctuary II* warship looms overhead. The second scene shows the Grandmaster crawling from wreckage, surrounded by natives of Sakaar, who have overthrown him. "I'm proud of you all… yay us!," says the Grandmaster, before judging the revolution a tie.

**Significance:** The arrival of Thanos' ship sets the scene for *Avengers: Infinity War*. Suddenly the Asgardians' hopes of a future on Earth seem a little less certain.

## EASTER EGGS (CONTINUED)

### DOWN UNDER

As most of the film was shot in Australia, and director Waititi is originally from New Zealand, there are many tucked-away references to Australia. For example, the spaceships are named for Australian cars: the Commodore, Statesman, Terrano, and Kingswood, all manufactured by the Australian company Holden.

### WHERE THE BEAST SLEEPS

In Hulk's private room, he has a bed composed of skeletal remains of a giant beast. This is the beast that he had to defeat in order to become the Grandmaster's champion.

### SAVAGELY ASTONISHING!

During his introduction to the arena, Hulk is described as "astonishingly Savage!" These are references to two titles the Hulk comics have had, namely *Savage Hulk*, and the anthology series *Tales to Astonish*.

### THE INFINITY FAKELET

As seen in previous *Thor* films, Odin's vault holds many treasures of the cosmos, including some of the most powerful items in the Marvel Universe. One of these items is the Infinity Gauntlet. However, it was later confirmed that Thanos was in possession of the true Infinity Gauntlet. When Hela explores her newly acquired kingdom, she comes across this relic and disregards it as "fake" before knocking it over.

### ROCK MONSTER

Korg, the rock monster played by director Taika Waititi, is a Kronan warrior. The Kronan made their debut in *Journey into Mystery* #83, which was the same issue that introduced Thor.

# BLACK PANTHER (2018)

## DIRECTED BY: RYAN COOGLER

STARRING: Chadwick Boseman (T'Challa/Black Panther), Angela Bassett (Ramonda), Letitia Wright (Shuri), Lupita Nyong'o (Nakia), Danai Gurira (Okoye), Daniel Kaluuya (W'Kabi), Florence Kasumba (Ayo), Forest Whitaker (Zuri), Winston Duke (M'Baku), Sterling K. Brown (N'Jobu), Michael B. Jordan (Erik Killmonger), Andy Serkis (Ulysses Klaue), Martin Freeman (Everett K. Ross), Sebastian Stan (James Buchanan "Bucky" Barnes)

In the aftermath of King T'Chaka's death, Prince T'Challa has returned home to Wakanda to assume the throne. He and Okoye, the General of the Dora Milaje, bring the spy Nakia back home to prepare for the ceremony. There is a trial by combat, where M'Baku, the leader of the Jabari Tribe, challenges T'Challa for the role of king. T'Challa wins, and is crowned king of his people.

One of his first objectives is to find and capture Ulysses Klaue, the man who, decades earlier, stole a cache of vibranium and sold it to the outside world. T'Challa leads a party to South Korea on a mission to apprehend Klaue. He's brought into custody by Everett K. Ross, now working for the CIA. The mercenary escapes, thanks to a man who wears a ring similar to the one that T'Challa's father used to wear. Wounded in the escape, Everett K. Ross is taken back to Wakanda by T'Challa, where he recovers quickly, thanks to their advanced technology and the expertise of T'Challa's sister, Shuri.

The mystery man is Erik Killmonger, the son of T'Chaka's brother, and T'Challa's cousin. Killmonger wants the throne for himself, so he can weaponize Wakanda's vibranium and use it to help liberate his oppressed brothers and sisters around the world. He defeats T'Challa in ritual combat (though T'Challa does not yield), and becomes king.

The wounded T'Challa is nursed back to health thanks to M'Baku, and his mother and sister. T'Challa, with the help of Shuri, Everett K. Ross, and the Dora Milaje, faces off against Erik Killmonger and the Wakandans who have sworn loyalty to him. While T'Challa leads the battle on the ground, Ross uses Wakandan technology to remotely pilot a fighter jet to prevent any vibranium from being exported. Together, they succeed in defeating Killmonger, and T'Challa once more becomes king.

## FIRST APPEARANCES OF:

Shuri, Nakia, Okoye, M'Baku

**01** Okoye and Nakia – dressed to kill. **02** T'Challa shows his combat skills. **03** Black Panther has a fierce presence

INTERVIEW

CHADWICK BOSEMAN

# The Once and Future King

Chadwick Boseman takes up the mantle of the Black Panther, not only an iconic Super Hero, but a socially and culturally relevant one. Here, the actor talks about what Black Panther means to him and audiences alike.

**A**s a comic book fan, what does it mean to you to be part of the Marvel Studios legacy?
It's fun for me to watch what it means to people. At times, in my head, I'll be like: *What does this do for the world? Is it actually valuable in the political climate, in the social climate we have?* And I have to say, yes! Not because it makes people escape, but I think when it's done right, it gives people hope. It lets people know that you can have a power beyond what you think you have. But even in having that, you're still vulnerable…

Those are important lessons, two different lessons, but important lessons for people to learn. And I've seen just what the movies mean to people who are suffering, who are not having the easiest times in their life. It'll make their day or week or month more meaningful if they can just meet Black Panther.

Were there any actors you were thrilled to work with?
The Chris's! Chris Evans I already was able to work with, but Chris Pratt, I knew him, but we had never worked together. We've talked quite a bit and I knew he was cool. But it was just great to be out there with him. Chris Hemsworth was really funny, really fun to be around.

What was it like at the big Marvel Studios 10-year photo shoot?
I was just laughing the whole time, and had a lot of inward giddiness in a certain way because I watched all these people in movies for my entire life. Laurence Fishburne and Sam Jackson and Michael Douglas. And

you're like, 'What am I doing here? What did I do to deserve this?'

And seeing them respond to you in that same favorable way and them being excited about your character and your movie, it's mind-blowing. It's a mind-blowing experience. It's mind-blowing to be up there with Stan Lee. These things that were in his mind are actually flesh and blood. He's like, "Here's my T'Challa.' But this comes from his head and comes from Kevin Feige's head. It's amazing!

And then you got Robert [Downey Jr.]. He started this. He's like HR for Marvel. He really is, you know what I'm saying? He really does keep it so we're not focusing on the machine, that we are focusing on the humanity.

What do audiences connect to with these films?
I think people enjoy seeing how the worlds clash, like how do the Guardians connect with Ant-Man or in Wakanda? It's almost like having a movie of cameos; that's what you do when you read comic books. You look for the meetings between Super Heroes. So it's a feast in terms of that!

I think the other thing is, it's great to see people win, but to see them lose, even if people don't die, you get the sense of exhilaration and joy from the loss. It's that emotional catharsis of trying to get to something that seems unbeatable and going through the pain of it, the tragedy of it. It's epic and classical. And so I feel like these characters are mythological characters in a lot of ways. But you have go through that sacrifice to live up to it. I think people will definitely enjoy all of that.

**04** Chadwick Boseman stands regal as Black Panther.

## EASTER EGGS

### PREYY ANYTHING

Killmonger's own Black Panther suit has a subtle leopard-print pattern, which is a reference to the character's trademark pet leopard, Preyy, from the comics.

### SONIC KLAUE

Ulysses Klaue's nefarious dealings with vibranium are what he's most famous for in the comics, but it's his sonic blaster arm that fans really remember (taking up the space where his left arm should be). Here, Klaue finally unleashes his prosthetic arm-disguised cannon. He even explains that it is based on a bit of Wakandan sonic mining equipment – a nod to the sonic cannon that it was in the comics.

### MAN GOES APE

M'Baku in the comics is better known as Man-Ape, an enemy tribe leader who dons a gorilla suit, physically embodying the white gorilla deity of his tribe. In the movie, the character is portrayed in a far less racially charged or problematic light, while still honoring the character's roots with the gorilla mask M'Baku briefly dons and his thick fur-covered armor.

### SON OF THE KING

Portrayed by South African actor John Kani in *Captain America: Civil War*, King T'Chaka's appearance was all too brief. Now audiences get to learn a little bit more about T'Challa's father, in a flashback where his 1992 counterpart is played by none other than Atandwa Kani, Kani's own son.

### BIRTH OF THE BLACK PANTHERS

While the setting of Oakland, California is close to director Ryan Coogler's heart (it being his hometown), there is a deeper connection to the film other than the fact it is home to Killmonger's origins. Just a few weeks after Stan Lee brought T'Challa to life in comic book form in 1966, the Black Panther party was founded in Oakland, and the two have been synonymous ever since.

### MERCY MAKES A KING

With the world watching, T'Challa is forced to stay his hand after defeating Ulysses Klaue in Busan. His powerful words, "Every breath you take is mercy from me," are not too unfamiliar, as fans will note it is the exact line he spoke to Namor in *New Avengers* #22.

### SANCTUM SPIES

When Killmonger enacts his plan to use Wakanda's weapons across the globe, most War Dog spies are hesitant to comply. However, three distinct cells are ready to attack: New York, London, and Hong Kong. These places should ring a bell as each of them holds a Sanctum Sanctorum, the hubs of mystical protection. Is there any significance here, or is it just a fun nod by Coogler?

## END CREDITS SCENES

King T'Challa – the Black Panther – shows us what it truly means to be a leader. For centuries, Wakanda has remained isolated from the world under the pretence of a Third World country, but as T'Challa learns, "more connects us than separates us... We must find a way to look after one another as if we were one single tribe." This mid-credits scene sees T'Challa address the UN as Wakanda plans to share its knowledge and technology with the rest of the world.

**Significance:** This scene – which was actually the film's original ending – is a nice nod in the 10th anniversary year of the MCU to *Iron Man* (2008), where Stark reveals his Super Hero identity to a gathered press conference. The scene also calls back to T'Challa's father, T'Chaka, addressing the UN shortly before he's killed in *Captain America: Civil War*.

In the post-credits scene, T'Challa's sister, the genius Shuri, has seemingly cured Bucky of his brainwashing, as he emerges from a hut relaxed and recuperated.

**Significance:** A certain Mad Titan is on his way to Earth, and the Avengers will need all the heroes they can get…

**05** Erik Killmonger is threatening as a warrior.

**06** Klaue takes aim during the frantic chase through the streets of Busan.

**07** Ryan Coogler directs Danai Gurira.

**08** The Dora Milaje are poised to strike against Killmonger.

**09** Nakia dons tribal green at Warrior Falls.

**10** Black Panther digs his claws into the chase.

# AVENGERS: INFINITY WAR (2018)

## DIRECTED BY: ANTHONY RUSSO, JOE RUSSO

STARRING: Robert Downey Jr. (Tony Stark/Iron Man), Chris Hemsworth (Thor), Mark Ruffalo (Bruce Banner/Hulk), Chris Evans (Steve Rogers/Captain America), Scarlett Johansson (Natasha Romanoff/Black Widow), Don Cheadle (James Rhodes/War Machine), Elizabeth Olsen (Wanda Maximoff/Scarlet Witch), Anthony Mackie (Sam Wilson/Falcon), Sebastian Stan (Bucky Barnes/Winter Soldier), Paul Bettany (Vision), Benedict Cumberbatch (Doctor Stephen Strange), Tom Holland (Peter Parker/Spider-Man), Chadwick Boseman (T'Challa/Black Panther), Danai Gurira (Okoye), Letitia Wright (Shuri), Chris Pratt (Peter Quill/Star-Lord), Zoe Saldana (Gamora), Dave Bautista (Drax), Bradley Cooper (Rocket), Vin Diesel (Groot), Pom Klementieff (Mantis), Tom Hiddleston (Loki), Karen Gillan (Nebula), Idris Elba (Heimdall), Benedict Wong (Wong), Gwyneth Paltrow (Pepper Potts), Benicio Del Toro (the Collector), Peter Dinklage (Eitri), Josh Brolin (Thanos)

The film picks up moments after the end of *Thor: Ragnarok*. The vessel that stopped the Asgardians' ship is revealed to belong to Thanos. The Titan has already acquired the Power Stone from the Nova Corps on Xandar, and has come for the Tesseract, an artifact that contains yet another Infinity Stone, the Space Stone. Loki had taken the Tesseract during the destruction of Asgard. To spare the life of Thor, his brother, Loki gives the Tesseract to Thanos, who kills him. Before Thanos destroys the Asgardians' ship, Heimdall sends Hulk back to Earth.

Banner arrives at Doctor Strange's Sanctum Sanctorum in New York City. Strange summons Tony Stark to join them, as Wong explains the true nature of the Infinity Stones and Banner fills them in on Thanos's plans. Thanos's minions arrive on Earth, looking to take the Time Stone from Strange. Abducted following a hard-fought battle, Strange is brought aboard one of Thanos's ships. However, both Stark and Peter Parker (in his guise as Spider-Man) stow away.

Meanwhile, the Guardians of the Galaxy follow a distress signal and encounter the debris of the Asgardian ship. They rescue Thor, who tells them he needs to travel to Nidavellir, where the Dwarves can forge a weapon capable of destroying Thanos. Thor, Rocket, and Groot travel to Nidavellir, while Star-Lord, Gamora, Drax, and Mantis travel to Knowhere, in an effort to grab the Reality Stone being kept by the Collector.

Back on Earth, Thanos' minions try to steal the Mind Stone from Vision, but they're beaten by the combined efforts of Scarlet Witch, Captain America, Black Widow, and Falcon. Together, they return to the Avengers' compound in upstate New York, where they gather with James Rhodes and Banner. They agree they must find a way to separate the Mind Stone from Vision so it can be destroyed; that delicate operation requires a trip to Wakanda, and the expertise of King T'Challa's scientist sister, Shuri.

Iron Man and Spider-Man manage to free Dr. Strange, and the three land on Titan, where they hope to take Thanos by surprise. There, they join forces with Star-Lord and the Guardians. Back on Earth, Thanos' minions prepare an all-out assault on Wakanda to obtain the Mind Stone.

Battling on separate worlds, the Avengers and Guardians come within inches of stopping Thanos, preventing him from obtaining all six Infinity Stones. But their efforts are in vain – not only does Thanos succeed, but with a snap of his fingers, he causes half the beings in the universe to cease to exist.

## FIRST APPEARANCES OF:

Eitri, Thanos's minions: Corvus Glaive, Ebony Maw, Proxima Midnight, Cull Obsidion

**01** Iron Man, Dr. Strange, Bruce Banner, and Wong prepare for Thanos' surprise attack on New York City.

INTERVIEW

## JOSH BROLIN

# Bearer of the Gauntlet

Appearing for the first time at the end of *The Avengers*, Thanos' approach has been known for a while. Josh Brolin discusses becoming the Mad Titan and leaving his mark on the Marvel Cinematic Universe.

**W**hich Marvel Studios films have been your favorites?
I'm just glad you didn't make me pick just one. I guess my number one choice would be the first *Iron Man* movie. It worked so well. For me, there's no better marriage of character and actor than that, and Robert Downey Jr. just got it. It all springboards from there, and now you can't think of another actor who could have played the role! So *Iron Man* didn't just set the bar, it also set the template for everything that's followed since. So that one has always been a favorite of mine.

Then there's *Civil War* – because there was so much drama in it, and there's a lot of friction too. And yet there's all these relationships that you have the history of, across all the other films. What is this guy, Captain America, gonna do? And that's the greatest thing, at least as an audience member, to me. It keeps you guessing.

And then most recently I saw *Thor: Ragnarok*, and I loved it. I love Chris [Hemsworth]. I think he, Cate Blanchett, and, obviously, Mark [Ruffalo], they're just great in it too. It really shows that they're all really enjoying their roles! And Cate Blanchett, wow! She's always been a favorite of mine too. She was great to watch. Hell, everybody was great! That was a good, really fun movie – it was a great hybrid of humor, action, and really fun acting.

**What sets Marvel Studios apart?**
It's the right collective. It's like, back when you used to have these theater collectives, and they're all working together putting this thing on and trying to find the color in everything, and the social significance, and all this stuff. And that's what makes the Marvel films stand out: that feeling that somebody gave a theater troop 500 million dollars by accident and they're all kind of adolescently, in

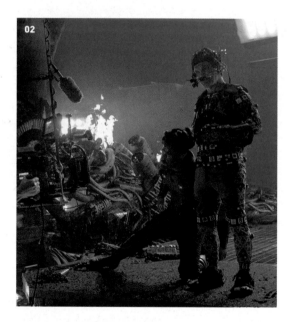

the most beautiful sense of the word, so into what might happen. They're like, "How can we paint ourselves into a corner," and then, "how will we find our way out?" Like, "wouldn't it be cool if that guy just suddenly did this," and it all comes together!

In this genre, the imagination of what you can create is limitless, which can be a really scary thing. You don't have to stay within full reality, and yet, somehow, Marvel makes all of it feel real for some reason. And I think it all goes back to this very identifiable place – the human perspective. So you can talk planets and universes and this and that and you can have these Infinity Stones and the big golden gauntlet and all this kinda big Earth-shaking stuff... but you never feel like it's so far away from you that you could never identify with it.

**02** Josh Brolin in his motion capture gear, dragging around Chris Hemsworth/Thor like a doll. **03** Josh Brolin as Thanos.

## EASTER EGGS

### DIRECTOR IN DISTRESS?

During the opening sequence, a distress call emanates from the Asgardian refugee ship, *Statesman*. The line was read by Sir Kenneth Branagh, the director of the first *Thor* movie.

### MAGICAL BANDS

Doctor Strange uses the Crimson Bands of Cyttorak to try and stop Thanos. This spell binds and subdues enemies and is frequently used in the Marvel comics.

### SEEING BLUE

Tobias Fünke from *Arrested Development* makes a cameo appearance, showing up covered in blue paint in the false Collector's vault, an illusion created by Thanos.

### WHO, HOW, WHEN?

The line "I'll do you one better: Why is Gamora?" from Drax was ad-libbed. Dave Bautista admitted that Chris Pratt gave him the idea for the line.

### INSANITY!

Thanos mentions how on his homeworld, Titan, he was called a madman. In the comics, a nickname for Thanos is the Mad Titan.

### SWEET GREEN REVENGE

In the first *Avengers* film, Loki was threatened by Stark with "We have a Hulk," shortly before the green giant came and left his mark on Loki. In *Infinity War*, when Thanos is threatening Loki, Loki informs Thanos, "We have a Hulk," before Hulk jumps into the fray.

### CHANGING NAMES

*Avengers: Infinity War* was originally supposed to have the subtitle "Part 1," to be followed by "Part 2" in the next *Avengers* film. The "Part 1" was dropped, and the next *Avengers* movie's name has yet to be announced.

### IT'S IN THE NAME

The name Thanos comes from the Greek name Thanatos, which translates as "Death."

### THE SHADES MAKETH THE IRON MAN

When Tony's nano-suit forms around him, he takes off his glasses. The glasses are made of the same nanotechnology, as they are absorbed into his new nano-suit.

## END CREDITS SCENE

The day the villains won. Thanos succeeds in his plan to collect all six Infinity Stones, and with a snap of his fingers he wipes out half the universe. On Earth, in the film's only credits scene, we see S.H.I.E.L.D. agents Maria Hill and Nick Fury talking about the global situation when a car careers uncontrollably in front of them. Nick realizes it's empty. A helicopter crashes into a building. And then Hill begins to crumble into dust. Nick rushes to the car to retrieve a pager-like device and sends a message before he too disappears. We zoom in to the device and on the screen, a new insignia flashes up: Captain Marvel! It teases the long-awaited debut of the eponymous character, played by Brie Larson.

**Significance:** The directors, Joe and Anthony Russo, considered not including a post-credits scene in *Avengers: Infinity War*, but it drives home the impact of Thanos' actions on ordinary people and provides a spark of hope in a very bleak ending. How Captain Marvel will fit into the MCU mythos and help the Avengers to beat Thanos remains to be seen…

**04** Captain America's team is ready when Vision is attacked by Thanos' minions.

**05** Falcon soars over the assault on Wakanda.

**06** Spider-Man's new armor is designed for traveling through space, with a built-in oxygen supply.

**07** Vision comforts Scarlet Witch after Thanos targets his Infinity Stone.

**08** Detailed model of Corvus Glaive, another servant of the Black Order and Thanos.

**09** A model for Thanos' right-hand man, Ebony Maw.

**10** Doctor Strange battles in New York to protect his Time Stone.

# ANT-MAN AND THE WASP (2018)

## DIRECTED BY: PEYTON REED

STARRING: Paul Rudd (Scott Lang/Ant-Man), Evangeline Lilly (Hope Van Dyne/Wasp), Michael Douglas (Hank Pym), Hannah John-Kamen (Ava Starr/Ghost), Laurence Fishburne (Dr. Bill Foster), Michelle Pfeiffer (Janet Van Dyne), Michael Pena (Luis), David Dastmalchian (Kurt), Tip "T.I." Harris (Dave), Walton Goggins (Sonny Burch), Judy Greer (Maggie Lang), Bobby Cannavale (Paxton), Abby Ryder Fortson (Cassie Lang), Randall Park (Agent Woo)

Scott Lang, who is under house arrest following the events of *Captain America: Civil War*, contacts Hope Van Dyne and Hank Pym after experiencing strange dreams about the Quantum Realm (where Janet Van Dyne/the original Wasp is trapped). Hank and Hope have secretly been building a tunnel to the Quantum Realm at their lab. The project is missing one final component, which they arrange to buy on the black market from Sonny Burch. Sonny double-crosses them, forcing Hope to don her Wasp suit and track him down. A masked figure, who is able to phase through objects, steals Hank's lab (which has been shrunk down using Pym Particles).

Hank and Hope, along with Scott, visit Hank's old colleague Bill Foster to ask for his help in locating the lab. They find it, but are captured by Ghost, who reveals herself to be Ava Starr, the daughter of Hank's old partner at S.H.I.E.L.D. When she was a little girl, Ava was in an accident which left her parents dead and rendered her molecules unstable. Foster reveals he is helping Ava, as he believes he can use Janet's Quantum energy to save her. Hank refuses to help, fearing the process could kill Janet.

Scott, Hank, and Hope escape back to the lab, where Scott is possessed by Janet (they formed a mental link when he previously entered the Quantum Realm), who provides vital information about the Realm. The police arrest Hope and Hank, and Ava steals the lab. Ant-Man helps Hope and Hank escape custody, and they find Ava and recover the lab.

Scott and Hope fight off Ava while Hank enters the Quantum Realm, but Burch and his men arrive, allowing Ava to escape. With Burch arrested, Scott and Hope take off in pursuit of Ava. Hank finds Janet and they successfully return from the Quantum Realm. Janet gives Ava some Quantum energy to temporarily stabilize her body.

Scott gets home before the FBI arrives, and his freedom is granted, while Ava and Foster go into hiding.

## FIRST APPEARANCES OF:

Dr. Bill Foster (formerly Goliath), Ava Starr/Ghost, Elihas Starr, Sonny Burch

**01** Ant-Man and the Wasp prepare for big trouble. **02** A crazed and desperate Ghost threatens Scott. **03** Hank Pym heads into the Quantum Realm.

INTERVIEW

EVANGELINE LILLY

# The Ways of the Wasp

The Wasp became the first female Super Hero to appear in a Marvel Studios film title – and actress Evangeline Lilly is very proud of that fact.

How have you found being a part of the Marvel Cinematic Universe?
I was actually giddy when I was walking out after I saw the first *Ant-Man and the Wasp* screening for the cast. I was just so proud and happy to have been a part of the movie. No matter what the critics would say or no matter how it would be received, I knew I would be proud of the film. Ultimately, as actors, I think that's the bottom line. You can do a tiny film that no one ever sees, but if you love it – if you love what you are a part of – then all the rest of the bells and whistles are irrelevant.

Were you excited to play Hope Van Dyne again?
There was actually talk of me being in *Captain America: Civil War*, and I was a little bit worried about that because she would have been introduced in a story that has nothing to do with Hope or her first taking on the mantle of the Wasp. I would have been nervous and a bit disappointed that the first titled female Super Hero in the Marvel Universe wouldn't get an origin film.

Marvel Studios called me to say, "We're not gonna use you in *Civil War* any more," and I thought, *Woo-hoo! That's great!* They said, "Let us explain, don't be upset – we really want to give her an origin film. We want to give her a full film and to really make a moment of this." And I was way ahead of them already and very eager for that to happen!

What is Hope's relationship like with Scott Lang in this second movie?
Well, she couldn't stand him for the majority of the first film – and then all of a sudden we're kissing in a hallway! So that was fairly simple and direct. In the second movie, they haven't spoken in a long time. Scott was in Germany in *Civil War* and he has been under house arrest ever since.

Paul [Rudd] and I have this delicate journey to go through together, emotionally, in this second film. It was

04

really challenging, and sometimes there wasn't a lot of breathing room for it because there's so much action in the film. It feels like acting acrobatics sometimes! But it works and it's groovy!

What makes this an "Ant-Man and the Wasp" movie?
The sequel mirrors what we did in the first film, to some extent. We're building the brand so that you can recognize it. You feel it – you know when you're watching an *Ant-Man* film in the same way that you know you're watching a *Star Wars* film. And we still want to surprise the audience and give them something fresh and new that they can be delighted by.

It's up to Peyton Reed to manage it all and balance everything, and I've always had utter confidence that he's doing it successfully. And that's one of the best things you can have as a performer: to have the utmost trust and confidence in your director. There's really nobody better to navigate through this second journey than Peyton.

**04** Scott Lang and Hope Van Dyne face an emotional journey in *Ant-Man and the Wasp*. **05** Evangeline Lilly took on "acting acrobatics" for the *Ant-Man* sequel.

## EASTER EGGS

### PAST PROJECTS

While Bill Foster's background in size manipulation is referred to in the film, we never get to see him power up as his comic persona, Goliath (who first appeared in *Luke Cage, Power Man* #24). However, the moniker has been previously referenced in the MCU – in *Iron Man 2*, Tony Stark asks J.A.R.V.I.S. for information relating to the projects "Pegasus, Exodus, and Goliath."

### WHO IS WOO?

Agent James Woo is actually older than Marvel Comics itself! He made his first appearance in 1956 in *Yellow Claw* #1, published by Marvel precursor Atlas Comics. The character worked with Nick Fury before joining the Super Hero team: Agents of Atlas.

### UN-EGGS-PECTED

Ava Starr/Ghost is the daughter of Hank Pym's scientist colleague, Elihas Starr. Comics fans will recognize him as the longtime enemy of Ant-Man, Egghead.

### LIKE FATHER LIKE DAUGHTER

Cassie Lang is eager to team up with her Super Hero dad and help people out. This could be a foreshadowing of the comics version of Cassie, who took up the mantle of Stature, a size-changing member of the Young Avengers.

### COMPANY TIES

Sonny Burch's ties to Ant-Man originate in the comics. He is the former chairman of Cross Technologies, the company founded by Darren Cross, the villain of the first *Ant-Man* film!

### WHAT'S THAT COMING OVER THE ANT-HILL?

Music has always been a big part of Marvel films. The *Ant-Man and the Wasp* trailer features the song "Ants Invasion" by the UK's Adam & The Ants, while the actual movie includes the band's song "Antmusic."

### LADY GHOST

The movie version of Ghost differs from the comics counterpart in many ways, mostly that she is a woman called Ava Starr. The comics version of Ghost is a somewhat creepy male, mostly known for being a regular enemy of Iron Man and, temporarily, a member of the Thunderbolts.

### SUPER VILLAIN POTENTIAL

Geoffrey Ballard, an FBI agent who works under Sonny Burch's thumb, doesn't have a huge role in the film, but comics fans may know his character by his alias, Centurion. His stint as a super villain saw him take on Super Heroes such as Iron Man and Goliath.

**06** There's something you don't see every day in San Francisco...

**07** The Wasp fends off attackers.

**08** The spooky Ghost.

**09** Ant-Man (or should that be Giant-Man?) searches for Sonny.

**10** Scott and Hope – suited and booted.

**11** Ant-Man and the Wasp fly into action.

## END CREDITS SCENES

In the mid-credits scene, with Hank, Janet, and Hope standing by, Scott has shrunk into the Quantum Realm to find particles that could heal Ghost permanently. Within moments, Scott's companions are turned to dust, victims of Thanos' snap, leaving Scott trapped...

**Significance:** As the first film in the MCU to be released post-*Infinity War*, fans were hoping for some much-needed answers. The mid-credits scene is certainly satisfying, but leaves us with so many more questions!

In the post-credits scene, we see the giant ant which covered for Scott's actions while wearing his FBI ankle bracelet continuing to do so by banging away on the drums.

**Significance:** Ant-Man's usual comedy style returns – but it's amidst the chaos following Thanos' attack...

08

09

10

11

MARVEL STUDIOS

CAPTAIN
MARVEL

# A NEW CHAPTER BEGINS...

## CAPTAIN MARVEL (2019)

### CAPTAIN MARVEL IS THE 21ST FILM IN THE MARVEL CINEMATIC UNIVERSE.

Written and directed by Anna Boden and Ryan Fleck, *Captain Marvel* stars Brie Larson as Carol Danvers, alongside Samuel L. Jackson as Nick Fury, Ben Mendelsohn as Talos, Djimon Hounsou as Korath, Lee Pace as Ronan, Lashana Lynch as Maria Rambeau, Gemma Chan as Minn-Erva, Clark Gregg as Phil Coulson, and Jude Law as Yon-Rogg.

The story is inspired by writer Kelly Sue DeConnick's run on Marvel Comics' *Captain Marvel* that began in 2012.

According to Brie Larson, "Marvel are at the high-stakes poker table, somehow coming out on top every time. We have fight scenes and lots of colors and explosions; but there's gonna be real heart, and real moments, and finding the truth in all of this."

"Marvel Studios' films feel relevant and political in so many ways. They tell stories of empowerment, of introspection, of learning to confront your ills and your dark side. I think that is why they are so popular." opines Jude Law.

"From this point onwards, Captain Marvel takes the lead at the forefront of the entire Marvel Cinematic Universe. This story influences everything that has happened in every movie you've aleady seen in the MCU," adds Kevin Feige, President of Marvel Studios, looking towards the future of the character.

**01** The Skrulls arrive on Earth. **02** Nick Fury and Goose chill for a moment **03** Captain Marvel's extraordinary powers manifest themselves.

# OFFICIAL MARVEL MOVIE SPECIALS!

## THRILLING NOVELS FROM THE MARVEL UNIVERSE

**Spider-Man: Hostile Takeover**
ISBN 9781785659751

**Captain Marvel: Liberation Run**
ISBN 9781789091656

**Avengers: Infinity**
ISBN 9781789091625
COMING SOON IN HARDCOVER!

**X-Men: The Dark Phoenix Saga**
ISBN 9781789090628
COMING SOON IN HARDCOVER!

**Marvel Studios' Thor: Ragnarok**
**The Official Movie Special**
ISBN 9781785866371

**Marvel Studios' Black Panther**
**The Official Movie Special**
ISBN 9781785866531

**Marvel Studios' Black Panther**
**The Official Movie Companion**
ISBN 9781785869242

## DELUXE "ART OF" BOOKS

**Marvel's Spider-Man:**
**The Art of the Game**
ISBN 9781785657962

**Spider-Man: Into the Spider-Verse:**
**The Art of the Movie**
ISBN 9781785659461

**Marvel Studios' Avengers: Infinity**
**War: The Official Movie Special**
ISBN 9781785868054

**Marvel Studios' Ant-Man and the**
**Wasp: The Official Movie Special**
ISBN 9781785868092

**Marvel Studios: The First Ten Years**
**The Official Collector's Edition**
ISBN 9781787730915

**The Art of Iron Man (10th Anniversary Edition)**
ISBN 9781785659508

**Spider-Man: Into the**
**Spider-Verse**
**The Official Movie Special**
ISBN 9781785868054

**Marvel Studios' Captain Marvel**
**The Official Movie Special**
ISBN 9781785868115

**The Road to Marvel Studios'**
**Avengers Endgame**
ISBN 9781785869259

**Marvel: Conquest of Champions: The Art of the Battlerealm**
ISBN 9781785659553

© 2019 Marvel

# TITAN-COMICS.COM

# TITANBOOKS.COM